HAS MODERNISM FAILED?

HAS MODERNISM FAILED?

Suzi Gablik

First published in the United States of America in 1984 by
Thames & Hudson Inc., 500 Fifth Avenue, New York, New York 10110
thamesandhudsonusa.com

First published in the United Kingdom in 1984 by
Thames & Hudson Ltd, 181A High Holborn,
London, WC1V 7QX
www.thamesandhudson.com

Second edition 2004

Library of Congress Catalog Card Number 2003112795

ISBN 0-500-28484-9
British Library Cataloguing-in-Publication Data

A catalogue record for this book is available from the British Library

Original design by Janet Doyle
Revised design by Liz Trovato

Printed and bound in the United States of America by Phoenix Color

For Melba and Manny

CONTENTS

A work of art is a gift, not a commodity. . . . Every modern artist who has chosen to labor with a gift must sooner or later wonder how he or she is to survive in a society dominated by market exchange. And if the fruits of a gift are gifts themselves, how is the artist to nourish himself, spiritually as well as materially, in an age whose values are market values and whose commerce consists almost exclusively in the purchase and sale of commodities?

Lewis Hyde, *The Gift*

PROLOGUE

Several years ago the cover of the University of Chicago alumni magazine featured the philosopher Richard Rorty announcing that "there is no Big Picture." I have never accepted this for one minute. My eye is always on the Big Picture—seeing how things fit together and interconnect. It makes me realize how much has changed since the original publication of this book. Twenty years ago, for instance, when I first began writing *Has Modernism Failed?* the art world was a recognizable place, in which people knew who the key players were, and everyone seemed to share a common vocabulary and perspective. Now everything is much more complex and diverse, so much so that no single individual—critic, analyst, or artist—can possibly be conversant with all of it.

At first, the prospect of rethinking old thoughts in a new way seemed like a rather daunting thing to do. Would these issues still stand up today? I wondered. But on rereading *Has Modernism Failed?*, the relevance and timeliness of its central theme struck me: where do spiritual and moral values fit in? It is still the case that art finds no direction from society—and that we are stuck in the paradox of an overload of stimuli but an absence of coherent purpose. If anything, the impenetrable pluralism of competing approaches is even worse now than it was then. Lewis Hyde's question, cited on page 9—"How is the artist to nourish himself, spiritually as well as materially, in an age whose values are market values?"—continues to offer possibilities for significance we can never exhaust. Certainly getting through the winter of our discontents today has become monstrously more difficult and contradictory than when I first hazarded into these realms.

Since this book was written, the art world has bifurcated into two completely different aesthetic paradigms which differ sharply in their views about the meaning and purpose of art. In the first instance are those artists who continue to proclaim the self-sufficiency of art—in defiance of the social good and any form of moral earnestness—and who don't really question the world view in which they find themselves. They merely swim in it like fish in water. These artists seek sameness and assimilation, not to challenge cultural assumptions, and their art tends to reflect the culture at large. In the second instance are those artists who want art to have some worthy agenda outside itself, some socially redeeming purpose. The battle lines over the proper function of art are more sharply drawn these days than ever, and the war is by no means over.

In Western culture, artists aren't encouraged to be integral to the social, environmental, or spiritual life of the community. They do not train to engage with real-life problems. Instead they learn to be competitive in the marketplace with their products. We live in a society in which all our products and institutions are defined and measured by this market ideology—none escape. Artists are identified as winners or losers in the success game, and "professional recognition," in the form of brisk sales and positive reviews, remains the pattern of thought that structures the internal rhythms of art making. For a long time I have been questioning these premises, always in the belief that it is possible to recover, if we choose, from the estrangements of Western civilization. But what makes anyone change their beliefs about something?

Human choice is one of the most powerful forces on the planet. We do have the option to give different beliefs authority and to withdraw from certain group beliefs. However, to construct one's life outside the numbing conventions of the status quo is a difficult undertaking. Anyone who wants to change the tides of where our civilization is headed needs first to look at the Big Picture—and then to become conscious of how profoundly they have internalized the values and dictates of the dominant paradigm. And after that, as Annie Dillard suggests, you go home and soak your feet. Because the task at hand, the task of cultural renewal, the task of choosing a different path in life, is very daunting. But it is an essential journey for anyone who is concerned about the future of this planet.

Twenty years ago, *Has Modernism Failed?* railed at the dangers of a culture which sees everything as an unregulated "market"—a culture that has a price tag on its soul and whose will to money is greater than its will to meaning, a culture with no controls or limits, and with no responsibility to create *values*. Now, for better or worse, we can only weep, like Albert Camus's Caligula, "because the world's all wrong."

Ever since that ghoulish blue-sky morning of mass murder and cascading buildings when Al Qaeda terrorists rammed two passenger jets into the twin towers of the World Trade Center, we have had a sense of the end of an era: its arrogance, complacency, inflation, and indifference to the world community. There is a special new knowledge of death and a feeling of vulnerability, as the world seems to be going down a blind alley.

During World War II, as described in Chapter Eight, the Dadaists and Surrealists responded to Auschwitz and the horrors they were facing by infiltrating the world with meaningless, aggressively absurd objects—white-haired revolvers, lesbian sardines, vaccinated bread, and flashes of lightning under fourteen years old. They felt that in such a catastrophic world, art no longer mattered. They felt impotent to change anything, and so the idea was to offer gibberish, as a form of mocking witness, to a civilized world that appeared to have gone mad. But there is also another story, somewhat more promising perhaps. During the same period of history, Albert Camus, a writer who worked in the French underground during World War II, saw as the "task" of his generation that of "keeping the world from destroying itself." As a result of living through what he described, in his Nobel Prize acceptance speech of 1957, as "twenty years of absolutely insane history," Camus actively embraced the struggle to construct "an art of living in times of catastrophe in order to be reborn by fighting openly against the death instinct at work in our history."

So here is the heart of the matter: the party line of art-for-art's-sake, which has long exempted art from any moral tasks, has also denied it any redemptive potential for social change. I have often quoted Clement Greenberg as saying: "I don't see art as having ever, in a real sense, affected the course of human affairs." Greenberg was an art critic with a brilliant reputation, an icon of modernist culture. In this single comment, he voices an attitude that has coalesced over time into the received aesthetic wisdom of an entire era. We are still living in the fallout from this philosophy. When Richard Serra states that art is "purposely useless" and has no utility function and doesn't answer to any program, why should we be surprised? The power of this narrative has been immense in our time; from its angle of vision, getting rid of the pedestal could indeed be seen as "the biggest move of the century," as Serra has claimed.

Has Modernism Failed? describes the core structures of modernity as an archipelago of four related forces: secularism, individualism, bureaucracy, and pluralism. In the two decades since the book was written, capitalism has mutated, and a new string has been added to the bow of modernity: the globalization of markets is now considered by many to be the most important economic, political, and cultural force of our time. As a result of transnational corporations consolidating their power, the market has become an even more pervasive force, deciding what's valuable and what's worthwhile, and imposing its logic and imperatives on all aspects of life. As the new hallmark of capitalism, the globalization phenomenon requires an additional chapter of its own. Two decades of accelerated globalization, driven by computer and data-processing technologies, have intensified the world's economic and cultural links, with the result that capitalism now defines the economic structure of the world. All of the issues I talk about have gone into overdrive. Whatever the weaknesses and malignancies of modern society (as described in *Has Modernism Failed?*), globalization has exacerbated them mercilessly.

In the new global economy, everyone is on short-term contracts, associations are more fleeting, nothing is done in the same way year after year, networks replace hierarchies and are constantly redefining their structures. "'No long term' is a principle which corrodes trust, loyalty, and mutual commitment," writes Richard Sennett, in *The Corrosion of Character*, a brilliant study of the relationship between culture and character. Social bonds in the workplace are being weakened; commitment is not put into practice. The new work ethic lacks sustained human relations and durable purposes. Values like trustworthiness, commitment, and purpose—all long-term virtues—are disappearing. As I write this, for instance, the ethos of corporate America, remains under a cloud of accounting scandals, the result of what Federal Reserve Chairman Alan Greenspan has called a culture of "infectious greed"—as witnessed by the frightening failure of accountants and stock analysts and company directors to protect the nation's retirement assets. "So where do moral and spiritual values fit in?" The question repeats, indulging in repetition the way that songs have refrains, or mantras "chant" their meaning into being.

As Sennett frames it, everything is now episodic—events, like layoffs, seem beyond anyone's control—and life is propelled by drift. In prioritizing economic growth at any cost, capitalism has begun to wreak its own havoc from within.

"By now people know," a journalist commented recently in *Time* magazine, "that capitalism is a spectacle of hope and greed and guts and guile, all racing toward the bottom line. That is its genius, but without guard rails, the whole contraption can take us over a cliff." Defining all agendas by money facilitates and preserves the functioning of the economic system, but it does not support other kinds of activities that do not generate income. The spiritual dimension of art has been replaced by something else: a set of rules and external standards that artists are expected to follow. I expect my own bias here is clear. My concern in this book has been to analyze the effects on culture of a growing subservience to a market fundamentalism that neither recognizes nor demands accountability. Institutions in the art world do not just reflect, they assist and befriend capitalism's "value-free" ideology, motivated by money. The visual arts in particular have been heavily implicated in these market economies. As in the larger world, the financial benefits go mostly to the chosen few who already enjoy them. Everyone else gets to divide up the crumbs.

Some time ago, I received a letter from a man living in Ohio, a self-described collage artist and writer, who also works full time as a social worker supporting people with disabilities. Keith Banner wrote that he now prefers making connections with disabled people—helping them to buy groceries, find places to live, purchase art materials, go to classes and museums, etc.—to being in academic culture, with its endless, esoteric theorizing about "texts" and "paradigms." And that in the course of his social work, he has discovered that many of these people with disabilities make wonderful art—often in secret. He and a friend began collecting their work and now organize exhibitions to show it. My books, he wrote me, have helped him to see himself in a new way as an artist, not "self-involved and struggling with made-up, phony aesthetic problems." Instead he has chosen to reach out and help people who are usually shut out of the conversation about art and culture.

"I am not sacrificing anything," he says, "and I am gaining everything." Reaching out, he says, cuts through the fakery and the pretense and allows art to be a huge part of his everyday life "without the excess baggage of artistic snobbery and professional drone." In my estimation, this is an artist who has become truly independent and self-directed—not manipulated by the coercive influence of others, mass consciousness, the media, or the art market. His work honors the world.

In the world of "professional" art, meatloaf footballs and pretzel butterflies may be curated to flamboyant acclaim. But the art world is much more wary of what Gregory Sholette calls "shadow practices" that make no attempt to display or distribute themselves through art-world institutions. In an intriguing essay called "Heart of Darkness: A Journey into the Dark Matter of the Art World," Sholette, a New York artist, writer, and curator who teaches at the Art Institute of Chicago, argues that there is a lot of "dark matter" in the art world, by which he means an "indefinite shadow realm" of unseen artistic activity that doesn't qualify as art for dealers, collectors, trade publications, auction houses—that is to say, the economically privileged who dominate and control the very idea of culture. The art elite tends to discount and exclude "dark matter" as being amateur, unskilled, and dilettante. Yet the line separating artistic value from other forms of artistic practice is often an arbitrary one. Art that neither requires capital to exist nor provides income to its creators is the one that gets discounted, however, as having no aesthetic significance.

Sholette describes how a limestone monument near his house in uptown Manhattan, which was built in 1913 to commemorate firefighters killed in the line of duty, became, after 9/11, the site of a spontaneous shrine, decorated with flowers, candles, and a bunch of soft children's toys piled up in a corner "like silent mourners." He notes that this is precisely the kind of informal arrangement that would be dismissed by serious artists and critics as "mere sentiment or kitsch," while a more fanciful and baroque display of similar toys in a prestigious art gallery by artist Mike Kelley becomes a high-end luxury item. What is wrong with this picture? Purveyors of postmodern culture have gone to a great deal of trouble to dismantle habits of meaning and social significance. And by this device, one often finds identical kinds of objects being valued in radically different ways. The blurred distinctions between art and non-art have always interested me. Mike Kelley's stuffed toys (unlike those at the shrine) have meaning, but only when viewed as art. Critics are willing to discuss them, but only because an artist such as Kelley has selected and installed them. Once this Rubicon is crossed, what was previously just a meaningless pile of toys then becomes a "purposely useless" but meaningful work of art. The process is infinitely repeatable, and hardly anyone will find it out of place.

Sometimes people think, when I talk this way, that I have a grudge against art objects. But it isn't true. (Personally I happen to enjoy Mike Kelley's work.) Or they think, given the problems of the world, I am suggesting that artists must try to do something about them. But the truth is, I don't think that either art or artists are what will save the world. Only a new way of being can do that—one that knits people together through an inspired ethos of generosity and caring, and a return to the root idea of what it means to make value-centered, moral choices. Without this, there is no way forward from here. The fundamental problem in the West today is the illusion of autonomy. It fails to recognize the interconnectedness of everyone and everything. And it ignores the well-being of the whole.

"There's 'good,' there's 'good at,' and there's 'good for,' in the sense of *good for* other people. In which of these ways should art and artists be 'good'?" asks Margaret Atwood in a recent book about writing, called *Negotiating with the Dead*. The question begs for an answer—though mine, I am aware, is a heretical one.

Art is an instrument. It can be used to make a difference to the welfare of communities, the welfare of societies, and to our relationship with nature. It is *good for* something. And this, in large part, should be the true measure of its success—not money, not favorable reviews, or an impressive list of shows, signaling a conditioned allegiance to art world approval. I have come to believe that true success manifests through a certain quality of awareness and an ability to live in an interconnected way, with compassion and responsibility. This means being able to step away from acquisitive and exploitative forms of individualism, and from the egocentrism of the present social order.

So here, then, is the heresy: I believe the truly significant product of an artist is his life. Creating oneself as an excellent person in all the activities of one's life, and in one's whole being, is the real work of art. The way I see things now, making the personality over in this spiritualized and value-oriented way is the only real antidote to the catastrophic and compromised world we are living in: shifting from egocentrism to what the Dalai Lama calls "altruistic mind." This altruistic quality of mind in Buddhism is also known as *bodhicitta*, or warm heart.

It has been said that "acedia," or not caring, is the most dominant sin of our culture today. If selfishness is indeed the virus that pervades the human species, then the high-level commitment of artists who want to use art to change life for the better can lead us in a new direction. Artists can be a saving grace. They can be teachers about how to take care—of our environment and our society. Many artists today have already taken roads more in line with this vision. We need this higher view, since we have been horribly sidetracked by the negative influences of a superficial culture that is spiritually illiterate and morally bankrupt.

I happen to believe, along with the Dalai Lama, that compassion, love, and altruism are not just desirable spiritual attributes; they are qualities that have become fundamental to our survival on this earth. They are the path to a more enlightened society. But these days, having your stock be high as an artist does not necessarily equate with goodness of character. As Margaret Atwood puts it: "If you're an artist, being a good man—or a good woman—is pretty much beside the point when it comes to your actual accomplishments... not being able to hit high C is not redeemed by being kind to dogs."

Well, of course, if you put it like that. It is best not to confuse the categories. The attitude Atwood describes so sardonically is quite real. It is just how we think. This is one cultural assumption I personally would like to hang upside down by the seat of its pants. As far as I am concerned, the 9/11 experience, and all that has followed upon it, suggest that we have now "outlived" the period of ethical neutrality in our culture, and the possibility of regarding our work as being beyond moral scrutiny.

My friend Carol Becker, an associate dean of the School of the Art Institute of Chicago, claims that what our culture really needs now, especially since 9/11, is to put community at the core of our species nature. "The collective project of our species," she states, "is to engage in its own conscious evolution beyond individual identity, difference, and nationhood. Its success can best be measured by how well we care for, protect, and value each other's lives." This is perfectly true: we have to embrace a more generous vision of ourselves than we ever thought possible. What I am asserting to round out this picture is that nothing less than a transformation at the core of our being—manifesting in the courage to act differently in the world—can save us at this juncture. The poet Rainer Maria Rilke has written: "Work of the eyes is done, now/go and do heart work." The complex task of nudging art away from the damaging consumerist philosophy that plagues it, and towards more compassionate and participatory cultural forms, remains a matter very much at hand.

CHAPTER ONE:
INTRODUCTION
The Waning of the Modern Age

Modernism—the term that has been used to describe the art and culture of the past hundred years—appears to be coming to an end. As we live through the unsettling moral and intellectual consequences of what the American critic Irving Howe has called the "decline of the new," it has become harder and harder to believe in the possibility of yet another stylistic breakthrough, yet another leap into radical form. In the complex transition from modernism into postmodernism, a new terrain of consciousness is being occupied—one in which the limits of art seem to have been reached, and overturning conventions has become routine. As long as we are willing to consider *anything* as art, innovation no longer seems possible, or even desirable. At this point in the breakup of modernist culture, as we draw away from it, we might do well to consider exactly what we have gained, now that the avant-garde has exhausted its tasks; and equally, what we may be losing as a result of its disappearance from the scene. It is not easy to represent to ourselves a whole that has been made up of so many changes and violent contrasts. Are we leaving behind us a period of success and resonant creativity, or one of impoverishment and decline? Has modernism succeeded, or has it failed? And now that pluralism is all the rage, does postmodernism offer even greater scope for freedom, or is it merely the effect of what Hegel called the bad infinite—which claims to comprehend everything but is, in reality, a false complexity that merely covers up a lack of meaning?

In 1952 the sculptor David Smith declared in a speech at Deerfield, Massachusetts, that "nobody understands art but the artist, because nobody is as interested in art, its pursuits, its making, as the artist." At that point there were only about fifty modern artists living in New York, who depended mostly on each other for support, and less than twenty galleries. Even as late as 1961, only about twenty-five artists of the older generation, according to the art critic Thomas B. Hess, were making what could be considered a "living" in New York. From the start, the mystique of modern art has always been that it is not generally popular, or even comprehended, except by an elite few. The art dealer and critic John Bernard Myers once asked Marcel Duchamp how many people he thought *really* liked avant-garde art, and Duchamp replied, "Oh, maybe ten in New York and one or two in New Jersey." That was back in 1945. More recently, a drastic expansion has taken place, and there are more people now concerned with art, either as producers or consumers, than ever before. There is currently a two-billion-dollar-a-year art market in New York City alone, and the 1982 Summer Gallery Guide, published by *Art in America,* listed 14,000 artists with gallery affiliations. The turning point is marked by no single event, but indifference and hostility have definitely given way to enthusiasm and wider audiences. Ambitious collectors and corporate buyers pursue works by high-priced artists as good investments, and today, a successful artist routinely expects a bulky income from his work. Museums are full to the point where people anxious to use them are often left standing outside. At the recent international Zeitgeist exhibition in Berlin, the scene was one of frantic buying and selling—one critic counted three dealers to every artist. The auction markets prosper: a single night's sale at Sotheby's can bring in over twenty million dollars, proving that the rewards of collecting are by no means exclusively aesthetic. And, as Calvin Tomkins commented some time ago in *The New Yorker,* given the choice, most artists would probably prefer to live at a time when art is in demand even if for the wrong reason.

In many ways, postmodernism seems not so much a revolution in styles as a surge of "rising expectations" on the part of everyone swept up by art's quantitative advance, and its piling up of vital possibilities. In a sense, everything that is good and bad in our present situation has its root in this general rise of expectations and escalating demands. And although the presence of a thriving market, and of galleries that are overflowing, suggests that the battle for acceptance has been decisively won, the world of art—now mediated by a bureaucratic megastructure that is impersonal, increasingly powerful, and potentially sinister—has become dangerously overinstitutionalized. This is no mere wild statement. Anyone who wishes can observe that at this point the art world pretty much divides up between those who manage and those who are managed. It is hardly an original observation to state that culture in postmodern society is increasingly "administered"—transmitted and controlled by means of corporate-management techniques, public relations, and professional marketing.

The world into which artists today are born displays features radically new to history. It is not like the world with which we were familiar during the high period of modernism. It is a world complicated by changes without parallel. Models and standards from the past seem of little use to us. Everything is in continuous flux; there are no fixed goals or ideals that people can believe in, no tradition sufficiently enduring to avoid confusion. The legacy of modernism is that the artist stands alone. He has lost his shadow. As his art can find no direction from society, it must invent its own destiny.

To the public at large, modern art has always implied a loss of craft, a fall from grace, a fraud, or a hoax. We may accept with good grace not understanding a foreign language or algebra, but in the case of art it is more likely, as Roger Fry once pointed out, that people will think, when confronted with a work they do not like and cannot understand, that it was done especially to insult them. It remains one of the more disturbing facts about modernism that a sense of fraudulence has, from the start, hung round its neck like an albatross.

Lack of faith in the authority and authenticity of what he does is not the only negative factor the modern artist has had to contend with. With art and artists breeding like bacteria under favorable conditions (it has been pointed out, for instance, that the education system in America fabricates as many graduate artists every five years as there were

23

people in fifteenth-century Florence), we are having to put up with an overload of stimuli and contradictory values, together with an absence of order and coherent purpose. This rise in quantity has in no way led to a rise in quality, though few have had the courage to say so. The overwhelming spectacle of current art is, at this point, confusing not only to the public, but even to professionals and students, for whom the lack of any clear or validating consensus, established on the basis of a common practice, has ushered in an impenetrable pluralism of competing approaches.

It is not easy any more to picture to oneself clearly what art is, or how it got that way, or more importantly, *how it can be justified*. What, finally, made modernism so different from other traditions? Renoir once wrote that works which were eminently collective and done for a community were possible in the past because painters possessed the same craft and had the same vision of the world, and the same faith—everyone learned to paint in the same way and had a religious feeling in common. Until the modern period, art and artists had always been imbued with a quasi-religious as well as a moral and social mission, and art was very much integrated with the social and spiritual orders. One of the deepest distinctions between other historical periods and our own is that whereas in the past, belief and hope permeated all human activity—and art had a clear consensus behind it—our own epoch is characterized by disbelief and doubt. Ideas that were once quite clear and satisfactory have become vague or irrelevant. And although many histories of modernism get written—scholarly analyses that investigate every cadence of style and manner—inevitably these fall short of giving the real curve of the thing: a reasonable account of why, in modern society, *art breeds mistrust*—why it seems calculated to provoke and disturb, and to make people uneasy. Certainly the problem of the popularity or unpopularity of art is inconceivable outside modern culture. The erosion of art's authority and credibility over the last fifty years, in a world that has become progressively more commercialized and career-oriented, must be linked, inevitably, with certain fundamental assumptions handed down to us by advanced capitalist society.

Since the nineteenth century, we have always classified art by schools and styles, viewing it as a history of forms that derive from some kind of dialogue with (or rebellion

24

against) previous styles and forms; but perhaps a classification by function would be better. For after all is said and done, what *is* the purpose of art? Art history, like all history, is woven of many discordant purposes; there is not just one. As John Cage once put it, "If there were a thousand artists and one purpose, would one artist be having it and all the nine-hundred and ninety-nine others be missing the point? Is that how things are?" In our society, artistic forms and purposes are no longer given by tradition; they cannot be taken for granted. The momentum of social change in the modern world has altered not only the nature of art, but also the psychological drives and motivations of those who shape it, to the point where we now find ourselves without ruler or compass in evaluating all these changes. To convey one instance of how much the common discourse flounders, I include the following edited extract from some *Art and Language* symposia that took place in Melbourne and Adelaide, Australia, in 1975. The transcripts were edited by Terry Smith, and I quote them at this length because they have the value of contemporary evidence. Many readers of this book will no doubt have observed or participated in such unfruitful exchanges at one time or another:

> HK (a member of the audience): What interests me is the question: What sort of things are you trying to achieve through doing art? . . . so among your set of aims when you do art are self-expression and communication?
> Artist-Participant: It is just like jumping off a tram, it's a vehicle for going somewhere. I could ask you why you are sitting on a chair. You are always going why, why, why? I enjoy it, that's all.
> HK: But you enjoy lots of things, going to the circus—what is special about your enjoying doing art?
> Artist: I agree art should not be put up on a pedestal. . . . My aims change all the time, they are different from drawings to paintings—the lecturers here are always at me because I haven't really got a style, they think I don't know what I'm doing.
> HK: How do you recognize when you're doing art as opposed to other activities?
> Artist: I don't. . . . Everything's art, there's just different ways of expressing it.
> HK: But that's robbing the word of any meaning. . . .

Artist: But art's a special language which doesn't contain words on your sort of level at all. Henry, what do you do? Who are you? . . .

HK: I'm a philosopher of science, my PhD is in mathematical physics. . . . I'm part of the public who is entitled to ask you what you think art is.

Artist: Isn't it better to just go on painting? We are going to finish up with everybody talking and no one painting. This is so boring!

HK: Well, if you don't find it valuable, you can leave. If you aren't enjoying the boredom, why don't you get a paintbrush and paint here?

One of the things I should like to achieve in this book is to bridge the gap in understanding that exists between people outside the art world and those within it. Although I have two different audiences in mind, I shall address myself—hopefully in a manner which is sympathetic both to the art and to those who have difficulty in understanding it —to anyone thinking seriously about art today but finding it hard to come to terms with some of the more conspicuous contradictions of the present scene.

Modern society has emerged in a single evolutionary arena —the West. It represents a systematic reversal of the values by which people in traditional societies have always lived. The emergence of modern art during the early decades of this century resulted from the coalescence of certain component ideas that form the basic structure of modern society: secularism, individualism, bureaucracy, and pluralism. These variables have formed the core of modernity; I shall need to examine the fate of art in relation to each of these great modernizing ideologies in turn, since they have had a determining impact on the modern social character and are what sets the modern world off from its predecessors.

By secularism I mean the despiritualization of the world, the modernist refusal of the sacred. It refers to that rationalizing process, tributary to the development of science and technology, through which the numinous, the mythic, and the sacramental have been, in our society, reduced to rags; and the gradual triumph, under advanced "late" capitalism, of a bureaucratic, managerial type of culture characterized by mass consumption and economic self-seeking.

The loss of art's moral authority—that authority which,

in a more enclosed social framework than ours, normally achieves legitimacy through its roots in tradition—is ultimately the true subject of all these essays. All culture is "situation-bound," and related to the circumstances that generated it. At this point in our history, art finds itself without any coherent set of priorities, without any persuasive models, without any means to evaluate either itself or the goals which it serves. To the postmodernist mind, everything is empty at the center. Our vision is not integrated —it lacks form and definition. Is it any wonder, then, that art has fallen prey to difficulties of legitimacy—or that, like a dark body which absorbs everything and gives out nothing, it should be undergoing what seems, by now, like a permanent crisis of credibility?

What artists expect for themselves has radically changed over the last fifty years as the lineaments of the art world have gradually shifted from an amorphous power structure into a clear-cut power structure irradiated with corporate values. The essays here are all concerned with the implications of this shift. In emphasizing the sociological character of art, this book stands in complementary and dialectical relation to my previous book, *Progress in Art*, which dealt with the cognitive character of art. My claim that art has a "progressive" history and structure (a claim which is not meant to imply moral or aesthetic improvement so much as a cognitive "growth" of styles) presupposes that the history of art, as a system of human interaction with the world, can undergo cognitive development similar to that in individuals. The history of art can be seen to ramify along many different lines of development, however, and is the outcome of several kinds of conditions. The present book is an attempt to take my previous analysis several steps further, by coming to grips with the modern era as a whole; it tries to grasp, describe, and analyze the psychological and social circumstances under which the art we possess has come into being.

As cultures change, so do the types of personality that are their carriers. The revised self-image of artists in postmodern culture means that art at this point requires some analysis in terms of its relation to contemporary character ideals. We have not arrived at our postmodern culture by accident—there is a discernible progression of events that has brought us to the current situation, which I propose to uncover. No proposition can be advanced about this subject, however, without my giving credit first to the central ideas I draw upon so unreservedly, and which I have taken so much to heart. Hardly any of these ideas originates with me: many authors have struggled with the problems I try to confront here. There may be no question of presenting new truths—and indeed, I am often no more than a medium in the transmission of insights to be found throughout the vast sociological and philosophical literature on modern Western society—but what I have done is to register the importance of these ideas by extending their application to present conditions in the art world. I cannot name individually all those whose thoughts have been crucial to the writing of this book—either quoted directly or used as background—but I should like to acknowledge my special obligation to certain authors whose works have been indispensable, and without whom, quite simply, my own book could not have been written. Among these are Daniel Bell, Peter Berger, John Dewey, Émile Durkheim, Erich Fromm, Anthony Giddens, Martin Green, Jürgen Habermas, Irving Howe, Herbert Marcuse, Lewis Mumford, Robert Nisbet, José Ortega y Gasset, Philip Rieff, Theodore Roszak, Edward Shils, George Simmel, Max Weber, and the co-authors of *Organizational America*, William Scott and David Hart, whose views on the rise of the "organizational personality" have been invaluable. With Scott and Hart I share the hope of producing a book that may be one more step in a de-conditioning process which may help people to become aware of the lethal dangers that arise from simply muddling along with the status quo.

Central to the later chapters are the ethical writings of Hannah Arendt, Sören Kierkegaard, Karl Jaspers, Alasdair MacIntyre, and Ralph Ross, writers for whom paying attention and thinking are moral acts. It is to their theories of human nature—the ideals they believe it is legitimate to seek—that this book is dedicated. There are many other authors who need to be acknowledged, too numerous to mention here. Their names will be found in the bibliography at the back of the book. Having written with a view to making difficult subjects accessible to all, I have tried to simplify things by avoiding footnotes and page references.

The content of each of these essays could not have been expressed, as in the thesis of *Progress in Art*, as a central argument whose proof is gradually adduced. Rather, it is a collection of arguments, organized musically around a continuous line of thought, with themes recurring in different keys that eventually orchestrate a particular point of view. Some people will respond to my account of the situation as an invitation to despair, but that is not my intention. It is more an uncovering of the social unconscious, a bringing to the surface of what is lying in the depths. The environment is merely a reflection of what is in us, and if the environment is to change, something in us must change. Nothing will change, however, as long as we remain unconscious of the fundamental forces which shape our lives, embedded as we are in the general cultural ambience. At this point, we need some fairly coherent organizing picture of what has been happening to us, so that we can weigh the costs of what we are doing. If we can penetrate to the true inwardness of a situation, if we do not dull our minds to its dangerous or unpleasant features, we are less likely to be seriously manipulated. We have the possibility of choice, once we see clearly what is going on. Basically, our need is for a full acceptance of the moral nature of so many of the problems that we face. Then perhaps we can find a way to pass through these conditions and transcend them, like Edgar Allan Poe's sailor who was able by careful observation as he sank into the maelstrom to understand the nature of the vortex, and thus could be carried up by the same spiral that sucked him down.

CHAPTER TWO: INDIVIDUALISM
Art for Art's Sake, or Art for Society's Sake?

Anyone trying to face the full reality of modernism can still get caught, even at this point, in the cross fire between its admirers (those who defend abstraction and art-for-art's-sake) and its detractors (those who believe that art must serve a purpose or be socially useful). The instability of art in our times, the confusion over what its purpose is and to whom, by rights, it should be addressing itself, have become, in recent years, a new Spenglerian darkness. In England, for instance, ever since the manifestations of anti-modernist outrage several years ago over the price paid by the Tate Gallery for a brick sculpture by Carl Andre, the snarling and ranting at certain kinds of late-modernist abstract art have hardly ceased; at that point the public, the critics, and David Hockney were all united in their savaging of monochrome canvases and the poor, scandalous bricks.

Those who defend modernism claim that art need not serve any purpose but should create its own reality. (The composer Arnold Schönberg went so far as to declare that nothing done for a purpose could be art.) Abstract art brought into being not only a new aesthetic style, but also a change of understanding regarding the very *raison d'être* of art itself. For the committed modernist, the self-sufficiency of art is its salvation. Aesthetic experience is an end in itself, worth having on its own account. The only way for art to preserve its truth is by maintaining its distance from the social world—by staying pure.

Quite deliberately, during the high period of modernism between 1910 and 1930, art cut itself loose from its social moorings and withdrew, to save its creative essence. The "dehumanization" of art that took place in the early decades of this century was very much a response to the artist's spiritual discomfort in capitalist and totalitarian societies alike. As Kandinsky put it, "the phrase 'art for art's sake' is really the best ideal a materialist age can attain, for it is an unconscious protest against materialism, and the demand that everything should have a use and practical value." In opposition to materialist values, and because of the spiritual breakdown which followed the collapse of religion in modern society, the early modernists turned inward, away from the world, to concentrate on the self and its inner life. If valid meaning could no longer be found in the social world, they would seek it instead within themselves. In the thinking of most early-twentieth-century artists, a work of art was an independent world of pure creation which had its own, essentially spiritual, essence. The artist saw himself as a kind of priest who divined the interior soul, or spirit. Kandinsky and Malevich and many other early modernists had a concept of life which was essentially transcendental, although not tied to institutionalized religion. "Art no longer cares to serve the state and religion," Malevich declared. "It no longer wishes to illustrate the history of manners; it wants to have nothing to do with the object as such, and believes that it can exist, in and for itself, without things." The attitude of art for art's sake was essentially the artist's forced response to a social reality he could no longer affirm.

This "inward turn"—the conviction that self-fulfillment was to be found in the encounter with oneself—inspired, in the early period of modernism, almost a theodicy of individual being; for many artists at that time abstraction was no less than an aesthetic theology. (Malevich went so far as to claim he saw the face of God in his black square, and Theo van Doesburg declared that "the square is to us what the cross was to the early Christians.") This notion of the artist as the last active carrier of spiritual value in a materialist world remained attached to all abstract art until the end of Abstract Expressionism. Mark Rothko claimed, for instance, that if the spectator read his paintings solely in terms of spatial and color relationships, then he had failed to understand them. "You might as well get one thing straight," he once told an interviewer. "I'm not an abstractionist. . . . I'm not interested in the relationship of color or form to anything else. I'm interested in expressing basic human emotions. . . . And the fact that a lot of people break down and cry when confronted with my pictures shows . . . they are having the same religious experience I had when I painted them."

The Abstract Expressionists considered themselves as still belonging to a spiritual underground in the heroic tradition of Kandinsky and Malevich. "So long as modern society is dominated by the love of property," Robert Motherwell wrote in 1944, "the artist has no alternative to formalism. Until there is a radical revolution in the values of modern society, we may look for a highly formal art to continue. . . . Modern artists have had to replace other social values with the strictly aesthetic." Even in its most abstract form, modernism was self-consciously dissident, setting itself against the social order and seeking its own freedom and autonomy. The bourgeois might identify himself in terms of a role requiring that he orient his life around money, but the modern artist sought his identity through opposition to a society that offered him no role he was willing to accept. The original meaning of the term avantgarde implied a double process of aesthetic innovation and social revolt; it took the form of an estranged elite of artists and intellectuals who chose to live on the fringe of society.

During the 1960s and '70s, however, late modernism began to cast up increasing instances of a self-referring formalism which denies to abstract art any kind of dissident role or meaning within the social framework. The stylistic innovations of the color-field painters who emerged around the critic Clement Greenberg—Helen Frankenthaler, Morris Louis, Kenneth Noland, Jules Olitski—are *only* aesthetic; they harbor no revolutionary pretensions, no religious fervor, no remnants of transcendence hung like clusters of ice on the very trellises of dawn. Greenberg in particular rejected the notion that there is any higher purpose to art, or any "spiritual" point to its production. Art only does what it does: its effect is limited and small. It is there to be aesthetically "good." Only the "dictates of the medium"—pure paint and the flatness of the picture plane—were held to be worthwhile concerns for painting. The very idea of content was taken to be a hindrance and a nuisance, and looking for meaning was a form of philistinism. The work is a painted surface, nothing more, and its meaning is entirely an aesthetic one. Stripped of all experience except a variety of painterly effects, and devoid of communication, however, it came to seem as if the pig in the pigment were missing (if I may borrow a favorite phrase from the writer William Gass). (As always, within our complex modernist scene, there are countervailing instances, exceptions to the rule of what I am saying—artists like Dorothea Rockburne in her *Angel* series, and Brice Marden in his *Annunciation* pieces, who continue to work close to the spiritual heart of abstraction.)

In a sense, then, for the committed modernist, the audience doesn't really exist. Barnett Newman always claimed that the real reason an artist paints is so that he will have something to look at. Once, when an interviewer asked the painter Clyfford Still whether he was concerned that his work reach the people, Still replied, "Not in the least. That is what the comic strip does." "Then you paint for yourself?" "Yes." Creation, then, is pure freedom, and art must justify its own independent existence, in contrast to what Baudelaire called the "forced labor" of professional life. For Still, and other artists of his generation, painting was the one act of ultimate freedom that could transcend politics, ambition, and commerce. The shrewd and self-effacing painter Jasper Johns, when he was asked early on in his career about the strong public response to his work, replied, "Well, I liked the attention. And I thought it was interesting that other people had a reaction to my work, because prior to that time I had assumed it was mostly of interest only to myself."

Such remarks would probably have mystified a Renaissance artist, who was always acutely aware of the particular patron who commissioned or bought his work. In *Lives of the Artists,* Vasari recounts how Michelangelo was beset on all sides by the public demands on his time and talents. Pope Clement wanted him to paint the walls of the Sistine Chapel; not only did he command him to paint the *Last Judgment,* he also determined that it should be a masterpiece.

Meanwhile, Michelangelo was also being pressed in a troublesome way to execute the tomb of Pope Julius. Then, in 1534, when Pope Clement died, Pope Paul summoned him to enter *his* service, and when Michelangelo refused, he became angry and said, "I have nursed this ambition for thirty years, and now that I'm Pope am I not to have it satisfied? I shall tear the contract up. I'm determined to have you in my service, no matter what."

Until we come to the modern epoch, all art had a social significance and a social obligation. To suggest that classical art was concrete but indentured (in the sense of the bondage attaching to a public task), and that modern art is free but abstract, is merely to point out that impulses to autonomy and individualism run counter to processes of socialization and tradition. It is to raise the question of whether the modern artist has enough power over circumstances, and the means within himself, to resolve this contradiction. No longer compelled to direct art toward the collective ends of society, he must—if he can—distinguish himself through outstanding uniqueness. But this emphasis on uniqueness has hindered the development of any collective style—in the face of such continuous questioning of all aesthetic modes and norms, modernism has never established a style of its own. Ever since the advent of romanticism in the nineteenth century, singularity has been the norm instead of, as in the past, mastery over technique, or skilled knowledge. The overarching principle of modernism has been autonomy. Its touchstone is individual freedom, not social authority. Liberation from rules and restraints, however, has proven itself to mean alienation from the social dimension itself; and perhaps the time has come when a more circumspect state of mind may perceive the need to strengthen art against its present condition of arbitrariness and fragility. As for the idea of freedom, we ought perhaps to examine it now more closely, to see whether it does not have a perilous shadow side that is leading only to "the dead end of a narcissistic preoccupation with self," which Christopher Lasch writes about with such pessimism.

The most widespread attack on modernism and on the whole notion of art for art's sake has always come from Marxists, for whom the idea of art's function as something purely aesthetic and individual, and without external attachments, is spiritually sterile and corrupt. It represents the devitalization of culture in the final stages of capitalism, when the social-functional aspect of art dries up because the bourgeois artist sees art as a private activity, as part of the quest for self-realization, and as a means for the release of the individual from traditional restraints. In these terms, to know oneself becomes an end, instead of a means through which one knows the world.

True art, Marxists argue, examines the social and political reality behind appearance and does not represent it abstractly, divorced from appearances and in opposition to appearances. Marxist aesthetics demands that art illuminate social relationships and help us to recognize and change social reality. For art to be a social force, it must have a wide audience, and it must pass judgment on the phenomena of life. It must have as its subject the social world. Marx constantly stressed that art has a human social reality and must be integrated in a world of meanings—*it is not a separate reality.*

Both these positions—art as the expression of the individual or as the fulfillment of social needs—seem equally intelligible, but their conflicting demands at this point frame a major crisis in our culture: truth to the self or truth to the values of society. The sensibility of our age is characterized by this dilemma. When we assume either of these positions, we feel, more and more, that we are somehow being mutilated. We cannot satisfactorily adjust ourselves to either position, since each of them renounces what the other retains. Nor can their contradictions be resolved unless we manage to achieve some consensus as to the role art actually plays in modern society. Certainly the notion of things having no meaning outside themselves—of being valuable for their own sake—is relatively new, and we must see ourselves as light years away from the time, for instance, when art was used as a pedagogic tool for the church to illustrate religious stories, in an era when few people could read or write. Now, as Andy Warhol says, artists make things for people that they don't really need.

As the most outspoken feminist/socialist critic in America, Lucy Lippard has always gone against the tide, arguing against formalism even when it was unfashionable to do so, and insisting emphatically on art with a message. Devoted herself to social and political issues, she has been one of the people seriously worried over the shift from radicalism into aestheticism that has characterized so much late-modernist art. Finding little middle ground between purely aestheticized art and social propaganda, she states, "I'd like all artists to be socially responsible whatever their art is. But it is not easy to figure out one's individual options between the extremes of total immersion in the queasy ethics of the art commodity system or furious rejection of all that it stands for."

Lippard was among the first to perceive a widespread disaffection among artists refusing to accept the restricted optic of art for art's sake, or the dominant control of the gallery system over our access to art. "While some artists have never questioned the current marginal and passive status of art," she writes in her most recent book, *Overlay,* "and are content to work within the reservation called the 'art world,' others have made conscious attempts over the last decade to combat the relentless commodification of their products and to reenter the 'outside world.' In the late '60s, after a period in which most avant-garde art was drastically divorced from social subjects or effects, many artists became disgusted with the star system and the narrowness of formal 'movements.' They began to ask themselves larger questions. When they looked up from their canvas and steel, they saw politics, nature, history and myth out there." Lippard's previous book, *Six Years: The Dematerialization of the Art Object,* was a chronological history of the period 1966–1972 when many artists, seeking alternatives to painting and sculpture which might provide a chastening corrective to the opportunism and callousness of the marketing system, developed new modes such as conceptual, antiform, earth, process, body, and performance art. (These will be discussed in chapter three.) Immateriality and impermanence were the main strategies used to dematerialize art so it would no longer be a "precious object" and thus alluring to the market—after all, you can't really sell an X trodden into dusty grass in Africa, or parallel chalk lines drawn for two miles in the Mojave Desert. The paradigmatic figure who provides Lippard with a model and occupies a place of honor in her writing is Robert Smithson, who was a pivotal figure in the development of "site sculpture" made for specific outdoor locations. His most well-known earthwork, the "Spiral Jetty," was a reclamation of disused land in the Great Salt Lake in Utah, and part of Smithson's importance for Lippard is that he was the one artist of his generation concerned with the fate of the earth, and the artist's political responsibility to it. Lippard first became politicized herself by a trip to Argentina in 1968, when she talked to artists who felt that it was immoral to make art in the kind of society that existed there. Since then, she has attempted, in all that she does, to reverse the modernist notion that you have to give up art to be in the world—or give up the world to be in art. In her own mind, there is no confusion as to whether the essential qualities of art lie in formal organization or in communication. She has passionately championed antinuclear and antiwar art, black and feminist art, and mass-produced art (in the form of printed matter and pamphlets)—in short, unself-centered art that is frequently indigestible by the market but still hopes to change the social system.

Similar debates over ethics and aesthetics, instigated by Marxist critics, took place in England during the late 1970s, eventually taking on the dimensions of a fierce civil war— much as, in *Gulliver's Travels,* the Big-endians and the Little-endians disagree over the proper way to break an egg. There has always been a tradition of hostility and suspicion toward avant-garde and experimental art in England, notably in the writings of Sir Ernst Gombrich, Sir Kenneth Clark, and John Berger (although I don't mean to suggest that any of these writers are linked by a common point of view). In the late 1970s, however, a new group of neo-Marxist writers emerged as the self-styled emissaries of cultural change. They expressed their indignation at the fecklessness of art under capitalism, while simultaneously proclaiming a crisis in contemporary art. Primary among these younger critics were Peter Fuller, a declared disciple of Berger's, and Richard Cork, former editor of *Studio International* and art critic for London's *Evening Standard.* Fuller's main claim is that art has become malignantly decadent under monopoly capitalism, and rendered impotent by advertising and the media, while Cork was especially active during the late 1970s in organizing exhibitions intended to present an alternative to modernism—"to rap the hegemony of painting over the knuckles," as he chose to put it. Both condemn the practice of formalist abstraction as an impotent form of intellectual elitism deprived of all possible meaning.

One of Cork's exhibitions, entitled "Art for Whom?" and held at the Serpentine Gallery in London in the spring of 1978, investigated the possibilities for artists of working within more "egalitarian" contexts than are available through galleries and the dealer system. Factories, hospitals, schools, libraries, pubs, football clubs, bingo halls, street corners, and town halls, according to Cork, are some of the options open to an artist prepared to forgo the artifice of the gallery ambience and willing to make art for ordinary people instead of for other artists. All the work exhibited the idea of community and group experience—a principle of social integration as distinct from the idea of personal self-expression. There were posters to save Bethnal Green Hospital from budget cuts, a work by Conrad Atkinson intended to bring to public attention safety issues with respect to iron-ore workers, a community scheme in which artists collaborated with children in Islington to design decorations for the walls of their school building. Taking us back to familiar, social reality was Cork's way of refuting what he considered to be the vacuous irrelevancies of late modernism's bricks and stripes—indeed, of all art which, like the owl, does nothing for a living but hoot.

Another point of Cork's is that critics should actually articulate a direction for art to pursue. One of his major complaints has been that most artists today want to retreat into some kind of inner sanctum, some private world of the imagination. It behooves the critic to intervene in this state of affairs, as a corrective measure, and to insist that "artists start to reverse their deadening tendency to address each other alone . . . without ever affecting the lives of those outside." The avant-garde, according to Cork, are united by their refusal to work for anyone apart from themselves, and cling like drowning castaways to the raft of what they quaintly call "creative freedom." Art must now discard the incestuous tactics of "stylistic infighting" and begin instead to convey meanings to "a public whose needs have been neglected for too long." It should belong once more to the mass of people rather than to a dwindling elite.

More recently, two lesser-known critics writing in *Art in America*, Don Adams and Arlene Goldbard, claimed that the neighborhood arts movement *is* in fact the basis of a new avant-garde. The community artist is the one type of artist at this point who has successfully resisted the values of the marketplace, offering up his skills in the service of the community. Only the community artist avoids the role of

"Sleeping Beauty," to which other kinds of artists in our society are condemned since they are always waiting to be "discovered." Their whole mode of life is devoted to preparing for this discovery. By not waiting each day to be discovered, the community artist is able to use art to transform the experience of a community. But, like the earlier avant-garde, they too are subject to the old debate of "Is it art?," since what they do may be too *useful* and therefore too much of a departure from the art-for-art's-sake norm.

I do not wish, myself, to be cast in the role of defending modern art against any of these one-sided views; but the fact is, I incline very much toward Marx's view that capitalist society, although it has gone beyond previous societies in economic development, and still further beyond them in science and technology, cannot hope to produce art equal to that of certain earlier forms of society—since capitalist production, because it stresses the profit-making value of art and turns it into a form of merchandise, is hostile to the spiritual production of art. (The Austrian economist Joseph Schumpeter once remarked, in a similar vein, that the stock exchange is a poor substitute for the Holy Grail.) Marx's main criticism of capitalism was that it crippled man because of its preponderance of economic interests; and he observed, more than a century ago, that "a writer is a productive laborer not insofar as he produces ideas, but insofar as he enriches the publisher who publishes his work." There was no "art world" in Marx's time, but the comment is equally apt in relation to contemporary artists and their dealers.

If the artist's role has become marginal in modern Western society, it is not because modern art is intrinsically defective; it is because our society has divested art of all but aesthetic value, just as it has deprived us of meaningful spiritual experience. If the disaccord between the artist and society in modern times is to be seen as a defect, it must be understood as a social problem, due not to any defects inherent in art, but to defects in the value system of modern society. Marx felt that the supreme value of a work of art —its ultimate aim and reason for being—is achieved along with and through other values: social, moral, and religious. But modern life has by now largely deprived us of belief in these values. As many writers have pointed out, the real problem of modernity has proved to be the problem of

39

belief—the loss of belief in any system of values beyond the self.

In traditional societies, the individual lives submerged in tradition which is, for him, immutable reality, transmitted from a venerable past; the individual does nothing on his own account, apart from the social group. Indeed, nothing is more terrible than to be cast out of the collective and to remain alone. It is hard for us to realize that modern Western notions of the individual—his selfhood, his rights, and his freedom—have no meaning in the Orient, or for primitive man. Self-seeking and the pursuit of profit are now seen as the natural characteristics of man, not as part of an historical process. Primitive art, however, is never personal. It doesn't reflect a private point of view; it isn't innovatory, or produced for a market. Medieval society, to cite another instance, placed art at the service of religion. The artist exalted the dominant values of his society, and society in turn recognized itself in an art that was expressive of its values. Both had a concept of man which was essentially a religious one. Religion, ritual, and art existed primarily to support the social order.

Modern capitalist society, on the other hand, has been largely an object of dislike by its artists. Our great art has almost never been socially celebrative; it has been overtly hostile or coldly indifferent to the social order. Not only have we been living for some time now without any shared ideal, we have largely been living without any ideals at all. The paradoxical truth of individualism is that it can only progress at the expense of the strength of common beliefs and feelings. Our one common belief at this point seems to be that no one can be made accountable: any form of limitation is experienced as a prison. These social and psychological facts have dislocated artists from their embeddedness in the real world. Gustave Flaubert (the patriarch of our alienation, according to Jean-Paul Sartre) wrote in one of his letters, "I'm frankly a bourgeois, living in seclusion in the country, busy with literature and asking nothing of anyone, not consideration, nor honor, nor esteem. . . . I'd jump into the water to save a good line of poetry or a good sentence of prose from anyone. But I don't believe, on that account, that humanity has need of me, any more than I have need of it."

For better or worse, modern consciousness is solitary, consequent to the disestablishing of communal reality. It is the most intense form of individualism the world has ever known. Modern life is lived in a world turned upside down, in which we are painfully aware of our separateness but have lost sight of our connectedness. This fact expresses, however paradoxically, the reality of our *social* situation: the most fundamental assumption of modernity, as Daniel Bell has pointed out, is that the social unit of society is not the group, guild, tribe, or city, but the person. That the contemporary bourgeois artist, as a result of these historical processes, sees his relation to art as an individual, and not as a social, relation is inevitable. Individualism and antitraditionalism are one and the same psychological force.

But does the isolation of the modern artist's work, or his personal loneliness, deprive his accomplishment of social meaning? Not according to Harold Rosenberg, who remarked long ago that "the individual is *in* society—that goes without saying. He is also isolated and, like Ivan Ilyich, dies alone. I find it no more noble or picturesque to stress the isolation at the expense of participation than to stress the sentiment for the social at the expense of isolation."

Marxists, on the other hand, reject the nonconformism and isolation of the modern artist as expressive of an abnormal and warped relationship to society—a form of negative interaction that implies personal moral and psychic degeneration. Modern art, because it is primarily an elucidation of the artist's inner world, is seen as too narrow, and incapable of expressing deeper social values. The English neo-Marxists have denigrated artistic freedom as a mere figment of bourgeois ideology and have attacked individualism as "the most tacit and virulent assumption in art." According to Peter Fuller, the contemporary artist's freedom is, in any case, illusory, since it is restricted solely to aesthetic questions. It is, he claims, "like the freedom of madmen and the insane; they can do what they like because whatever they do has no effect at all. . . . They have every freedom except the one that matters: the freedom to act socially." It is easy enough to attack the restless vanity of capitalist culture under the umbrella of radical Marxist aesthetics, but the fact remains that the great art of recent centuries has emerged largely under capitalism, and not under socialism.

Socialist systems have not been notable for achieving better art than market systems—they just grant the individual less freedom and restrict his powers of choice.

There is a crucial sense, however, in which Peter Fuller is right: if the artist has total freedom—if art can be anything the artist says it is—*it will also never be anything more than that.* The real crisis of modernism, as many people have rightly claimed, is the pervasive spiritual crisis of Western civilization: the absence of a system of beliefs that justifies allegiance to any entity beyond the self. Insistence upon absolute freedom for each individual leads to a negative attitude toward society—which is seen as limiting to one's projects, and ultimately constricting. We need not be Marxists to perceive the extent to which overweening narcissism, compulsive striving, and schizoid alienation have become the dark underbelly of individual freedom in our society. There is no doubt that even freedom can become desolating, that after a while, even the artist may not know what to do with it. In a word, we can no longer really avoid the whole question—so poignantly put by Peter Berger—of whether the modern conception of the individual is a great step forward in the story of human self-realization, or whether it is, on the contrary, a dehumanizing aberration in the history of mankind. At the very least, it is a phenomenon with a very short history that has not been essential in the past to human survival, or to a rich human culture—and with the backfire of scrutiny, we may yet come to see that it may prove inimical to both.

If the great modern enterprise has been freedom, the modern hubris is, finally, the refusal to accept any limits. If previous societies were formed on the limitations of man's destiny, our own suggests a definition of life which meets with no limitation whatsoever, and allows the individual, as a result, to abandon himself to himself—without any communal obligation that might regulate freedom and prevent it from becoming narrow and selfish. Our present predicament rests on whether we can find some way of balancing the desire for individual freedom with the needs of society —and whether, at this point, we are able to shake ourselves free of the modernist notions of uninhibited individualism and endless innovation, which have become a sterile monotony. There is no doubt that the consequences of exaggerated individualism—which disposes the individual to isolate his own interests from the mass and to leave the rest of society to look after itself—are being questioned on all sides. In the words of Daniel Bell, "We are groping for a new vocabulary whose key word seems to be limits: a limit to growth, a limit to the spoliation of the environment, a limit to arms, a limit to the tampering with biological nature." The real question, however, is whether we will also set a limit to the exploration of cultural experiences. Can we set a limit to *hubris?* The answer we give to these questions, according to Bell, could resolve the cultural contradictions of capitalism, and of its deceptive double, the culture of modernity.

Once we have seen how much art and society are correlative, perhaps we can find a position of equilibrium between the two extremes of Marxist socialism, which tends to ignore the aesthetic character of art, and an aesthetic formalism that treats art as socially unconditioned and autonomous. What is required is some sort of reconciliation—not a fixture at either pole. Even just specifying these extremes, setting them side by side as I have tried to do here, is enough to evoke all the difficulties attached to giving any workable definition—that is, one that might be held more or less consciously by everyone—as to how art should function in modern society or what it is for. Socialist art deprives us, on the whole, of formal and aesthetic qualities, being strong on message but often weak as art; whereas formalism obliterates meaning and purpose, often to the point of transforming meaninglessness itself into a primary content. Neither of these roads has been able, in our own day, to reach the transformational center from which redemption comes; but this is another question, of which more later.

A few artists working today have managed, all the same, to move beyond a socially indifferent formalism toward a more community-oriented framework, without any sacrifice at the level of aesthetic quality. One of these is John Ahearn, a New York artist associated since 1977 with Colab (Collaborative Projects, Inc., a group of young dissident artists who came out in favor of art as a radical communications medium rather than as a circular dialogue with the traditions of the past). Ahearn casts life-sized portraits of neighborhood groups and families in the South Bronx, which succeed in combining a powerful level of aesthetic expression with an energizing social meaning: the conviction that both art and society concern everyone. For Ahearn, sculpture is a form of art which can appeal to a wide public. He has set up working "studios" in unusual places like elementary schools, nursing homes, and bowling alleys, where he casts directly from live sitters—who nearly always receive a sculpture in return for their participation. The finished portraits are luxuriously hand-painted; imbued with an almost visionary radiance, they express a passionate openness to the world, and love of it.

One of the intentions of the Bulgarian-born Christo, famous for "wrapping" objects, buildings, and landscapes, is to stimulate others to collaborate in his art. But, as he says, after the strains and complexities of dealing with the world which the realization of any of his major projects entails—the construction of *Running Fence,* for instance, involved half a million people—having an exhibition in Soho seems like a holiday. The artist, Christo claims, used to be the man who put things together, until the Victorian age, when they became specialists, like horse-painters. Today the art world manipulates all art into a make-believe reality. His own projects are far from specialized; they take place outside the art world and often require environmental studies, legal battles, material production in factories, and the mobilizing of thousands of volunteer labor forces. Getting it all together is a collaborative effort on the part of many people, and energy for the work is drawn as much from the community as it is from the artist himself. When *Running Fence* was constructed in California, a twenty-four-and-a-half-mile length of white nylon had to be stretched across land belonging to ranchers, most of whom were initially hostile to the project. Part of Christo's "work" involved winning them over; it took nearly a year to convince sixty families to let their land be used, but in the end they gave him not only the desired permission but also immense support, promoting press conferences themselves to defend the project publicly.

The collision of so many highly contradictory currents at the end of the 1970s produced the cultural whirlpool from which a pluralist ethic, with its appetite for all-encompassing multiplicity, was able to emerge. Pluralism is one way the dialectical contradictions of modernism get erased. Now, as we advance into the 1980s, we find ourselves surrounded by all the disorder of our unresolved intentions—

at the same time that we are besieged by all that is possible. But, as I shall argue in a later chapter, the danger is that when everything becomes art, art becomes nothing. For how can we ever succeed in forming a concept of something which is so totally open that all attributes apply to it equally? The 1980s so far have led us to the discovery that the craving for unlimited freedom may be ultimately entropic. It deprives art of direction and purpose until, like an unwound clock, it simply loses its capacity to work.

CHAPTER THREE: ANXIOUS OBJECTS
Modes of Cultural Resistance

The phrase "anxious object" was first used by the critic Harold Rosenberg to describe the kind of modern art that makes us uneasy because of uncertainty as to whether we are in the presence of a genuine work of art or not. Faced with an anxious object, we are usually challenged, and may even find ourselves baffled, disturbed, bewildered, angered, or just plain bored. The difficulty is to discover *why* this is art, or even *if* it is art. Consider, for instance, one of Jasper Johns's painted bronzes. How do we know if what we are seeing is a sculpture or just an old coffee can with somebody's paint brushes in it? Can we find the answer to the question by simply looking? Anxious objects often contribute to the confusion of one thing with another. What Johns has done is to "reconstruct" the Savarin coffee can that holds his paint brushes by first casting the real objects in bronze and then painting the cast to look exactly as the objects looked before he cast them. The result is so true to life that a genuine confusion arises as to its identity. By creating a situation of tension and ambiguity, anxious objects raise questions about how we know what we perceive. They force us to overcome our routine responses and to develop finer and more discriminating ones. Perception, we learn, depends on more than just looking—it depends on our ability to interpret what we see.

People are trained, in modern bureaucratic societies, to

carry out monotonous routines. A person whose whole life is spent performing a few repetitive tasks becomes mechanized in mind; hardly ever breaking through the surface of his routine, he finds little opportunity to exert his understanding, judgment, or imagination. The critical faculties grow dull and perception is blunted, hardened by a crippling sameness. This sort of collective trance, with its automatic and reflex responses, usually remains constant: the conformist mind does not change, or grow with experience, unless something happens to disrupt it.

Difficult and disturbing art acts as a countertendency to this leveling process—precisely because it disrupts our habits of thought and strains our understanding. By being subversive of perception and understanding, art can break through stereotyped social reality and produce a counter-consciousness that is a negation of the conformist mind. Indeed, it is only through *estrangement*—according to Herbert Marcuse—that art fulfills its function in modern society. Its "negating power" breaks the false automatism of the mechanical mode of life.

An anxious object, then, is instantly recognizable by its subversive tendencies. Usually, it has not been made in the manner in which we expect art to be made. Often it touches the limits of credibility, putting itself just beyond the boundary of what is acceptable. The quintessential anxious object—arguably the first of its kind—was Marcel Duchamp's urinal which he entitled *Fountain* and submitted to the Independents' Exhibition in New York in 1917, under the pseudonym of R. Mutt. More than any other object, it tests our assumptions about art—and our ability to find out whether all that professes to be art really *is* art. The urinal demands an answer to the question "Why is this art?" But Duchamp, the most agile and adroit ironist in the business, preferred to pose a different question: "Can one make a work which is not a work of art?" Always inclined to push things to their philosophical, moral, and aesthetic limits, and intrigued to find out *exactly what it is* that makes something a "work of art," Duchamp picked an ordinary, commonplace object—a manufactured and mass-produced urinal—chosen precisely for its *lack* of aesthetic qualities, and exhibited it as art. It was like handwriting in the sky that sketched out the pattern of things to come: art would never be quite the same again. What shocked people most was the utter artlessness of the object, and the fact that no "work" was involved. "Works" of art, in Duchamp's view, resulted from the artist's intentions, not from craft or skill, which required repetitive actions that could be learned by anybody. Real artistic invention depends on something else—on a departure from all routines, on gestures that destroy our expectations. To imitate or repeat oneself meant that one risked developing a "style," by which one could then be known or categorized. The main thing, therefore, was to contradict oneself as much as possible. Having thus transformed an ordinary object into art, Duchamp then set about reversing the procedure. He declared that a painting by Rembrandt should be used as an ironing board.

What Duchamp demonstrated was that art could be made out of anything. There is nothing about an object—no special property or function—that makes something a work of art, except our attitude toward it, and our willingness to accept it as art. One of the more subversive aspects of the readymade was that it undermined the usual motives for acquiring art—urinals can be acquired by anyone in quite ordinary ways. There are enough of them around so that one might just turn up anywhere—as indeed one did. A urinal quite similar to Duchamp's was found, by chance, in Alaska, where it had been mysteriously abandoned in a woods sixty miles from the nearest highway. The urinal was found by a former student of a young Conceptual artist, Ronald Jones, who lives and teaches in Sewanee, Tennessee. Knowing of Jones's special interest in Duchamp, the student had the urinal brought out by helicopter and shipped to Sewanee—at which point the reversals of the modernist plot become even more stunningly complex. If Duchamp started it all by appropriating a found object and turning it into a work of art, Jones followed suit by making a work which was a "found" replica of Duchamp's found "original." The whole enterprise, undertaken apparently in a spirit of pious imitation, survives by virtue of the artist's wit and talent for parody. When Jones exhibited *his* urinal, he appended two texts to the installation. The first was a statement by Duchamp himself, extracted from a letter to the Dadaist Hans Richter. Written in 1961, it read, "I threw the urinal into their faces as a challenge, and now they come and admire it as an art object for its aesthetic beauty." The second text was a statement by the aesthetic philosopher

George Dickie: "But the *Fountain* has many qualities which can be appreciated—its gleaming white surface, for example. In fact, it has several qualities which resemble those of Brancusi and Moore."

Balanced as if on a knife edge between brilliance and absurdity, the urinal has served as a trigger for many subsequent works—for example, the artist Bruce Nauman photographed himself in 1966 with water spouting from his mouth and titled the photograph *Portrait of the Artist as a Fountain.* One of the earliest examples of an artist appropriating someone else's work or idea was Robert Rauschenberg's *Erased Drawing,* done in 1953. Rauschenberg asked the painter Willem de Kooning to give him a drawing so that he could erase it. De Kooning eventually agreed. The drawing Rauschenberg was given had been made with grease pencil, ink, and crayon, and it took him a whole month, and forty erasers, to succeed. Rauschenberg then exhibited the erased drawing as a work by himself. More recently, a young New York artist called Sherrie Levine—also interested in appraising our notions of art's uniqueness and originality, and following closely on the heels of Duchamp and Andy Warhol—has begun duplicating the photographs of famous photographers such as Walker Evans and Edward Weston, which she then exhibits under her own name. Levine lays no claim to traditional notions of "creativity." By willfully refusing to acknowledge any difference between the originals and her own reproductions—by expressly denying their rightful authorship—she is addressing her work in a subversive way to the current mass cult for collecting photographs, and their absorption into the art market as one more expensive commodity. Obviously, ideas like these are "successful" as a negation of commodity-oriented culture only until commodity culture succeeds in accommodating even these "pirated" creations and turning them into yet another salable item within the framework of institutionalized art-world distribution—at which point they become more parasitic than critical, feeding on the very system they are meant to criticize.

Modernism has thrown up many aggressively absurd forms of art that simply cannot be understood outside their corrosive relation to the contradictions that capitalist society poses for the artist: namely, the fact that art's value tends to be defined, not by its spiritual, intellectual, or emo-

49

tional content, but by its economic worth. Duchamp understood, perhaps better than any other artist in our time, that once shaped by the market, art is on a collision course with itself, and its subversive value will be distorted, buried, or misappropriated. His own solution was to go underground and let everyone believe he had given up making art in order to play chess. That way he was able to avoid becoming "occupationalized," or "professionalized." Somebody once asked him why he didn't work, and was against working, and he replied, "Lazy people like myself cause the least trouble." The truth was that he was secretly engaged for twenty years in making one of the great masterpieces of our century—the large environmental work *Étant Donées*—which only came to light after his death and is now in the Philadelphia Museum.

If Duchamp recoiled from the idea of ever repeating himself, the opposite is true of Andy Warhol, who is absolutely fixated on the notion of doing the same thing over and over again. Warhol first began painting serial paintings of Campbell soup cans in 1962. They were banal, morally weightless images, but they managed to turn our ideas about painting inside out like a glove. By mass-producing silk-screened pictures on an assembly line in his Factory, with sometimes as many as fifteen people filling in the colors and stretching the canvases, Warhol, too, was subverting the notion of the handmade, "original" work of art. In Warhol's work, there aren't any originals—there are only reproductions. In place of the unique work, Warhol substitutes a plurality of copies. "I used to have the same lunch every day, for twenty years, I guess," he explains, "the same thing over and over again." Sameness, boredom, and above all, repetition are what, for Warhol, express the structures and modulations of consciousness—so we should not be astonished to learn that he once owned eight cats all named Sam. By making no distinction between what is genuine and what is counterfeit, Warhol makes even the authorship of his work appear dubious. "I think somebody should be able to do all my paintings for me," he says. "That's probably *one* reason I'm using silk-screens. I think it would be so great if more people took up silk-screens so that no one would know whether my picture was mine or somebody else's."

The attempt to deprive works of their "aura," or uniqueness, as a means of deflecting their transformation into a consumer object was a primary aim of the Conceptual art that emerged in the New York and European art worlds toward the end of the 1960s. Many Conceptual works did not exist as objects at all, but as ideas only. "Once you know about a work of mine," declared Lawrence Wiener, "you own it. There's no way I can climb into somebody's head and remove it." And Robert Barry, in 1968, stated, "The world is full of objects, more or less interesting; I do not wish to add more." These artists, together with Joseph Kosuth, were among the first to work in this new mode of art as idea, or information, which opposed other, more traditional aesthetic orientations like painting and sculpture. Reducing art to pure thought, Barry produced a *Telepathic Piece* in 1969 that consisted simply of the statement "during the exhibition I will try to communicate telepathically a work of art, the nature of which is a series of thoughts that are not applicable to language or image." Such works deny not only the motive, but even the possibility of acquiring the work, since there is, quite simply, nothing to acquire. Kosuth's classic early piece *One and Three Brooms,* for instance, has no object which, properly speaking, serves as the art. The work consists of a proposition about real objects and their corresponding representation in images or words: a real broom has been hung on the wall, together with a photograph of it and a dictionary definition of the word "broom." Kosuth has stated that he thinks art should be more like pure science or philosophy, which are totally self-sufficient, don't depend on audiences, and have no commodity or investment value. In the case of Art and Language, an international group of Conceptual artists with whom Kosuth was associated for a time, their primary practice took the form of conversations, discussions, and modes of linguistic and cultural analysis. (More recently, however, they have taken to painting mock Neo-expressionist pictures by holding on to the brushes with their teeth.)

To exhibit a concept, according to the French artist Daniel Buren, does not really dispose of the art object, since it comes to the same thing—one is simply replacing the object with a concept. Buren seeks, himself, to create work that is neither an object nor a concept. Since 1966 his work has consisted of vinyl sheets made up of white and colored vertical stripes and glued over surfaces such as walls and fences, either indoors or outdoors. In *Watch the Doors Please,* done in 1982, Buren covered the exterior double doors of 165 railroad cars belonging to the Illinois Central Gulf Railroad with stripes. He refers to the composition of these works as "zero" (there is none). The internal structure of each piece (the vertical stripes) stays the same and is continuously repeated; only the external structure varies, depending on the work's location or "frame." A giant two-story window in the Art Institute of Chicago which overlooks the train tracks serves as the frame for *Watch the Doors Please.* Posted next to the window is a schedule telling the times when the trains are due to pass. At that moment, the work may be seen; after that, as the train travels away from the museum frame, it is exposed to many more viewers and, in a sense, becomes anonymous public property. Buren, too, is trying to overcome the exclusivity of private ownership, which he perceives as standing in direct contradiction to the public (and collective) function of art.

It must be said that many late-modernist works of the past two decades have violated the "time-honored forms" in order to shift the meaning of creative activity away from the value of the finished product. The intention of such works has been to remain relatively free from the realm of consumerism, the exigencies of the market, and fluctuations of supply and demand. In changing the very nature of art, however, they have exacted a fundamental adjustment in our ideas about structure, permanence, durability, and boundaries. At the furthest extreme, the Frenchman Yves Klein (who pioneered Minimal and Conceptual, as well as Performance and Body art) presented the idea of art as *nothing,* emptying a Paris art gallery of furniture, painting it white, and exhibiting the empty space as art. Three thousand people came to the opening. On this occasion, emptiness became a "prime object," in George Kubler's sense— that is to say, a prototype of great generating power able to provoke a revolution in perception. It wasn't that one thing simply replaced another, but that by inversion, the context (in the form of the gallery itself) became the art. To borrow again from William Gass, it was as if the moon had been made to jump over the cow, or the fiddle play the cat. Conceived in this way, art is no longer a *thing*—its vitality lies elsewhere than in an ultimate substance. But if even the Void can be art, so can its opposite, as when the French sculptor Arman filled a Paris gallery with two truckloads of rubbish in 1960; or when Walter de Maria, an American sculptor, filled a New York art gallery with 220,000 pounds of earth. In this case, the outrageously worthless was soon converted into the expensively prestigious, since the artist's dealer (functioning as the Director of the Dia Foundation, a trust fund which functions both as a support foundation for artists and as a tax loss for the de Menil family in Texas) then bought the entire building in which the installation had been made, in order to keep it there permanently. Another sculpture of de Maria's (also sponsored by the Dia Foundation) consisted of a gigantic hole drilled one kilometer deep into the ground in Kassel, Germany, in 1977. A brass rod one kilometer long was inserted in the hole, which was then capped with a metal plate, rendering the work permanently invisible, known only through its absence. This venture, which cost the Dia Foundation $300,000, prompted the critic Robert Hughes, well-known for his skeptical turn of mind, to hail the vanity of such an undertaking as an "epigram of waste"—a criticism likely to seem scandalous to an artist who sincerely believes he is dealing in thunderbolts. Art like this, however, is bound to encounter difficulty in getting itself believed. For we are up against two different attitudes of mind—one reserved for the artist's creative activities, in which he makes violently antisocial works intended to defy the ruling ideology, and one for his personal interaction with society, in which he does not resist that ideology. Art which lodges itself firmly in a world of superabundance and excess—and ultimately, of superfluity—can hardly serve as a model of cultural resistance. In its conspicuous identification with the cash-nexus, it is hardly the negation of our consumer culture, but is its complement, implementing the established order rather than breaking with it. The estrangement effect has changed into a luxury occupation.

Other artists, concerned with a more ecological approach, have used gravity, chance, stones, water, and even walking as materials from which to make art, often choosing remote sites for their work in order to circumvent the artificial environment of the art world. Robert Smithson liked pouring tons of asphalt, mud, or glue down the slopes of gravel pits or eroded cliffs in order to study its movement. Smithson inevitably chose swamps, slag heaps, and industrial wastelands as sites for his earthworks, partly because he felt museums were too much like graveyards—they neutralized the power of art by confining it and removing it from the world. "A work of art," he wrote in 1972, "when placed in a gallery loses its charge and becomes a portable object or surface disengaged from the outside world." Smithson was one of those artists who foresaw, quite early on, that "the investigation of the apparatus the artist is threaded through would become a growing issue."

In contrast to sculptors who prefer industrial materials and produce enormous, indestructible monuments, the English artist Richard Long uses only natural materials, and also chooses unusual locations for his work. Although he makes some works which can be exhibited in galleries and sold, his outdoor sculptures—a stone line laid out in the Himalayas, or a stone circle in the Andes—are not subject to possession or ownership. They are not even objects added to the landscape, just simple rearrangements of what is already there. His art, he claims, "is about working in the wide world, wherever, on the surface of the earth. . . . Mountains and galleries are both in their own ways . . . good places to work." His real concern is to show that radical and robust art can be made in a simple, quiet way and with minimal intrusion of the artist's ego. "In the sixties," Long claims, "there was a feeling that art need not be a production line of more objects to fill the world. My interest was in a more thoughtful view of art and nature, making art both visible and invisible, using ideas, walking, stones, tracks, water, time, etc. in a flexible way. . . . It was the antithesis of so-called American 'Land Art,' where an artist needed money to be an artist, to buy real estate to claim possession of the land, and to wield machinery. True capitalist art. To walk in the Himalayas . . . is to touch the earth lightly . . . and has more personal physical commitment, than an artist who plans a large earthwork which is then made by bulldozers. I admire the spirit of the American Indian more than its contemporary land artists. I prefer to be a custodian of nature, not an exploiter of it. My position is that of the Greens. I want to do away with nuclear weapons, not make art that can withstand them [like Michael Heizer]." Art of this sort is ultimately political even though it deals with things that are not in the least political.

The nomadic, ecological way of thinking is not bound to

any particular style. The American artist Robert Janz makes chalk drawings in the street, for instance, that are completely ephemeral—rain eventually washes them away. His circular shapes, drawn on the outside of the Victoria and Albert Museum in London, slide gently out of alignment as they traverse obstructing angles in the architecture. Work like this subverts all our notions about what art should be: measurable by the constancy and quality of its effects and by its substantial presence in space and time; the embodiment of an exemplary craft; a meaningful message about the world. How much do we insist on these conditions? With their own kind of modesty, these drawings assume an ecological obligation not to pollute the world with more objects. To condemn the artist for his failure to conform to traditional criteria of skill or permanence is to quite miss the point, since he rejects those values and proposes radical new ones instead. As does Jacqueline Monnier, an American artist living in France, who makes kites, conceived not for galleries or museums, but to live in their natural habitat of sky and sea. "The sky," she writes, "is really a virgin space. The blue, you feel you can go on and on in it." For Monnier, kites are a form of collaboration with nature. It is the kite tails which enact her dream of movement and color in the sky. Sewn and glued into festive and lacy patterns from simple materials like crepe paper, rayon, or cellophane, they quite literally sculpt the air, each one like a bird with its own characteristic plumage. If the wind is strong enough, some kites will take up to eleven tails. Watching them ascend is to experience a lovely, suave, fluid electricity in the sky. More recently, Monnier has been making kites which uncoil like ancient marine reptiles under the sea, where, by contrast, they are very slow moving, having a specific gravity similar to water.

In Australia several years ago, I had occasion to meet an artist who also works directly in the landscape, using only natural materials like twigs and stones, gently modifying the site but never dominating it. When I visited John Davis in his studio in Melbourne, he showed me a number of fragile, devotional objects he had made. They resembled aboriginal ceremonial sticks or shamanistic prayer arrows. I wanted to buy one, but it turned out that, with the exception of major pieces to museums, Davis was not eager to sell his work. He preferred to give it away, or to barter it for other people's work, as an homage to the gift-exchange practices of primitive cultures, which for them was an important part of social life. Since he earns a good living through teaching, he doesn't need to sell his art, which leaves him free, on occasion, to give it away, because that is closer to what he believes in. (The American artist Joseph Cornell also had the habit of giving away his boxes; but as they increased in value, this became more difficult to do, as they were always in danger of being sold or stolen.)

There are many artists who have perceived the danger of becoming a mere agent of our social tendencies and have tried, personally, to draw back from it by making work that is in some way unsuitable for immediate consumption. But since consciousness is, in the end, largely determined by the interests of the established society, and since the individual who has a career in mind will obviously be eager to promote his or her own cause, ideals must be bent to suit the demands of the times. "As artists we have sold off inspiration to buy influence," the Minimalist sculptor Carl Andre has said. "We have always had the historical choice of either lying through or living through our contradictions. Now through the genius of the bourgeoisie we have the chance to market them."

Andre began stacking and piling beams in 1961, but a bit later he turned to arranging bricks, laying them out in a repetitive manner horizontally along the floor. He made his sculptures hug the ground. It was a way of getting away from all the accumulated verticality of more traditional forms. "The engaged position is to run along the earth," he said. "My ideal sculpture is a road." A row of bricks can be made by anybody—nor does it seem wildly salable. Still, it gets sold, and for a high price, even though, like the urinal, it shows no visible signs of "work" or craft. All the parts are equal and interchangeable; there is no composition, no construction or carving, no expressiveness. For this reason, Minimal art is boring to many people, who consider it not informed by any creative struggle or search. But boring the public—as the critic Barbara Rose pointed out about this new art back in 1965—is one way of testing its commitment. "The new artists seem to be extremely chary," she wrote. "Approval, they know, is easy to come by in this seller's market for culture, but commitment is nearly impossible to elicit. So they make their art as difficult, remote, aloof and indigestible as possible."

It is undoubtedly a truism that different types of art are produced by different societies, but modern Western society does seem to be unique in regarding its art as a commodity to be sold in exchange for money, prestige, and power. The idea of making art for profit appears when spiritual, moral, and economic life begin to be separated from one another with the development of foreign trade, and it marks the distinction between a gift-giving society and a market society. Aboriginal society, for instance, did not perceive art in terms of its commercial value—no pre-industrial culture ever did. Art was a living thing, not something external to the artist to be sold at a profit. It was a means of coming into contact with the life-force of nature. Sacred designs were painted in secret and revealed only in ritual—guarded from women, strangers, and the uninitiated, and often burnt when they had served their purpose. Today, bark painting flourishes only in Northern Australia, and under Western influence, the paintings are now made for a market of art dealers who sell them in urban centers, mostly to tourists.

In his book *The Gift,* Lewis Hyde claims that the way we treat a thing can sometimes change its nature. He also argues that in its fundamental nature, art is a gift and not a commodity. So it is hardly an accident, given the detached nature of commodity exchange (in contrast to the bonding power of gifts), that we have called those nations known for their commodities "the free world." The phrase doesn't seem to refer to political freedoms; according to Hyde, it merely indicates that the dominant form of exchange in these lands does not bind the individual in any way—to his family, to his community, or to the state. It is only when a part of the self is given away that community appears. Commodity systems have their own sort of growth, but they bring neither the personal transformations nor the social and spiritual cohesion of gift exchange. Indeed, for those who believe in transformation (either in this life or in another), ideologies of market exchange have become associated with the death that goes nowhere.

As present-day modern culture becomes increasingly depersonalized and administered by bureaucracies, some artists have reacted by producing works whose extremities, peculiarities, and individualizations are so exaggerated that they cannot be reduced to monetary equivalents. In some cases they are using their own bodies as a medium—the aggressive intimacy, for example, of Vito Acconci putting a match to his breast and burning the hair off his chest. On another occasion, in a work called *Trademarks,* Acconci bit himself all over, as much of his body as he could reach. He then applied printer's ink to the bites and stamped bite prints on various surfaces. One reason art like this makes us anxious is that it violates our sense of boundaries; no distinction is made between public and private events, between real and aesthetic emotions, between art and self. For Acconci, *all* experience is aesthetically provocative. He has said that the end of a performance, because of the extremity of its stress, might even be the development of a handicap.

But performance as a life-event becomes ambivalent as art: Yves Klein, for instance, in 1960, dressed in a business suit and necktie, leaping from the window ledge of a building into a Paris street. Just as Malevich in 1917 declared himself to be the "President of Space," proposing his new objectless paintings as an analog of cosmic space, Klein thought that bodily flight into space was the most revolutionary of all acts. He thought the whole universe was his stage. "Today," he wrote, "anyone who paints space must actually go into space to paint, but he must go there without any faking, and . . . by his own means: in a word, he must be capable of levitating." Is it theater—or is it real? On the occasion of the photograph, Klein did jump from the second story, but was caught in a tarpaulin by friends. (The photograph was then doctored and the tarpaulin removed.) On several other occasions, however, he made similar leaps without any protection.

Along with notions of impermanence and inaccessibility, then, we also find artists making use of violence, self-mutilation, and high personal risk as acts of provocation that force the viewer to examine his or her own emotional responses. Our society is one which devalues suffering, hardship, and adversity in favor of comfort, efficiency, and occupational success. Almost as if by compensation, certain artists have felt compelled to bring us back to an experience of the negative, as when the California artist Chris Burden crawled half-naked across broken glass. Much of Burden's early work centered on physical and psychological endurance tests, and sometimes even disfigurement. In a work called *Transfixed* (1974), Burden had himself nailed to the roof of a car. "Inside a small garage on Speedway Avenue," he wrote, "I stood on the rear bumper of a Volkswagen. I lay on my back over the rear section of the car, stretching my arms onto the roof. Nails were driven through my palms into the roof of the car. The garage door was opened and the car was pushed half-way out into Speedway. The engine was run at full speed for two minutes. Then it was turned off, and the car was pushed back into the garage. The door was closed." In an even earlier work done in 1971, Burden had himself shot in the left arm by a friend holding a .22-caliber rifle standing twelve feet away. Asked why somebody in his right mind might want to do such a thing, Burden explained, "It's something to experience. How can you know what it feels like to be shot if you don't get shot? It seems interesting enough to be worth doing it." Once the editor of a now-defunct art magazine entitled *Avalanche* asked Burden why he considered that his work was art. And Burden replied, "What else is it? It's not theater. . . . Getting shot is for real. . . . Lying in bed for twenty-two days. . . . There's no element of pretense or make-believe in it. If I just stayed there for a few hours or went home every day to a giant dinner it would be theater. . . . Now I know what to expect. The unknown is gone. I mean, there's no point in ever getting shot again."

Mounted on a red velvet plinth, the nails that were driven through Chris Burden's palms were subsequently sold in a New York art gallery. It is but one of endless instances that demonstrate how art-world priorities now get into every bit of our behavior—and how what ends an individual seeks are very much a matter of the kind of social structure in which he finds himself. The artist believes that he has done well. He does not perceive his art as being distorted, or its effectiveness impaired, in order to conform to the practices of a money culture. Or, if he does perceive this, he believes it is in his own interest not to care. Once an institution like the market system has been accepted as legitimate over a long period of time, it inescapably acquires a life and momentum of its own. It then produces a "false consciousness," whereby we all uphold and participate in this set of arrangements, believing them quite indispensable to our well-being. But we can see how advanced art today is no longer a cause, and contains no moral imperative. Even if the individual artist is persuaded that these social arrangements are on the wrong track, he cannot (as Goethe once said in a similar connection) be required to gain insights that threaten his life-conditions, as long as a chance at economic and sociological security is also involved. But the estrangement effect withers once it is absorbed into the dynamics of consumption, and the purpose it originally set out to serve is falsified at its core.

The Australian artist Mike Parr, who lives and works in Sydney, has often used real violence in his work as a tactical measure—in an effort to make it impossible for the audience to retreat into passivity about what was happening by assuming it was only a theatrical experience. In an early work called *Leg Spiral,* he tied a gunpowder wick around his leg and set it afire. Forced to cope with a direct assault on its understanding, the audience becomes implicated and involved. Parr turns the emotional urgencies of his personal life into material and means for a powerful kind of performance art. A more recent tableau consisted of him chopping off his arm with an axe. Parr's left arm is congenitally unformed, and much of his early work dealt with his feelings about this disability. The arm he chopped off was an absolutely lifelike prosthesis made out of latex and stuffed with animal livers. Afterwards, his sister and wife removed the remains, and his sister attached in its place a pink knitted arm she had made. The pink arm has not been put up for sale, nor have the remains of the prosthesis.

The now unrelenting pressure on art to be "successful" usually ends up requiring that insight be separated from practice. Success and status are compliance-producing forces, inducing us to interpret art in the fashion provided by our culture, and to cling tenaciously to certain ways of behaving. Someone not brought up in our society, and therefore not automatically committed to those goals—the Taiwanese-born performance artist Tehching Hsieh, who entered the U.S. illegally in 1974, would be an example—finds himself under less pressure to compromise. Economic success and security, comfort and pleasure, were not part of his upbringing in China and have not formed his outlook.

The performances of Tehching Hsieh last for a whole year. His first long work, entitled *Cage Piece,* involved remaining in a cage he built in his loft on Hudson Street for one year (1978–79). "No read, no write, no TV, no radio," he states. Following upon that was a time-clock piece (1980–81) in which the artist punched a time clock every hour on the hour, twenty-four hours a day, for one year. In 1981 he began a third work in which he set himself the task of remaining entirely *outdoors* for a whole year, in Manhattan. During this time, Hsieh documented his activities, photographing himself daily. He never once went indoors, or entered a building, subway, train, car, or tent. He slept in doorways, parking lots, or under the Brooklyn Bridge. "Each day outside I spend like bum," he has stated. "But piece is not a bum. Is an artist. . . . I choose to do this. I plan it, I am prepared. Outdoors is my symbol for outside world. People can hurt you, the winter can hurt you. Is more dangerous. Outdoor piece is symbol for human struggle in world. . . . In New York much freedom, but to be good artist freedom not enough, you need discipline." Hsieh makes his performances last for a whole year because he believes that a year symbolizes a whole life—to do a piece for only a week is to make a separation between his art and his life, and thus to feel himself perform. For Hsieh, it is crucial that his life and his art be one thing—his medium is real time, and real deprivation. And the more difficult his art becomes, the more it challenges him to touch his own limits and potentials, to see what point in himself he can reach. The Viennese psychoanalyst Otto Rank once wrote (in 1932) about the artist: "His calling is not a means of livelihood, but life itself . . . he does not practice his calling, but *is* it." Today, however, whatever we do, we are supposed to do for the sake of "making a living," and the number of people, especially in the artistic and intellectual professions, who might once have challenged this view has notably decreased.

Obviously, art does not do the same thing, epoch after epoch, merely changing its style; its function varies enormously from one society to another. Art has always interacted with the social environment; it is never neutral. It may either reflect, reinforce, transform, or repudiate, but it is always in some kind of necessary relation to the social structure. There is always a correlation between society's values, directions, and motives and the art it produces. Modernism, as we have seen, has cultivated its objects largely as a mode of cultural resistance—as antidotes to a bureaucratically administered and overrationalized way of life. The art of the last fifty years, in particular, has been dominated by a style of perception that is difficult, willfully inaccessible, and disorienting. Anxious objects do not elicit the standard, cherished responses to art—rather they seem to openly contradict traditional functions of uplifting, redeeming, and reconciling, substituting instead the disequilibrium of shock and doubt. Their primary function has been to create a critical consciousness; but more often than not, this critical function has simply disappeared, as mass bureaucratic culture assimilates potentially subversive forms of art and deprives them of their antagonistic force by converting them into commodities.

Because we live in a consumer economy, where the cash value of things has become their primary value, it is difficult for us to imagine another way of life, or mode of thought, than ours. Looking over the vast range of human achievement, however, makes it quite clear that our values are not the only standards by which art can be understood and judged. In primitive societies, the incentives for making art are chiefly non-economic; they arise from tradition, and from religious considerations. There is no art of revolt. It is only in some societies that artists are specialists. Carving a temple gate or making a set of ritual masks in Bali, for instance, is done anonymously, nor can the Balinese social structure be seen as a collection of individuals vying for status and prestige. The American Indians and the Australian aborigines valued art for its magical powers; and among the Kalabari of southern Nigeria or the Maori of New Zealand, sculptures are intended as "houses" for spirits, to achieve some control over them. In China the great painters lived like hermits, in the solitude of nature, from which they drew their inspiration. They avoided the life of the court, and gave away their pictures.

Clearly our modern Western world is only one of a large number of possible worlds, but the assumption nevertheless remains that modernity is not only distinctive, but superior to all that has preceded it. Modernism's freedom and autonomy, however, which would have been inconceivable in previous societies, is becoming increasingly hazardous and ambiguous as it collides head on with our society's distortions of artistic and cultural life. Just how successful the strategy of estrangement has been in liberating the artist from becoming yet another commodity-producer—of aesthetic "goods"—or in establishing any real alternative to the corporate value system, is open to question, since, as I have also tried to show, most of that art is ambivalent all the way through. Whether the modern artist's alienation can still be considered a socially productive resource or whether he, too, seduced by the promise of a little affluence and a more comfortable life, sold out to the system long ago, is an issue still to be resolved. The paradoxical nature of co-option has been nowhere better stated than by Hans Haacke, an artist who is preoccupied with tracing corporate systems of power and influence, and who uses his art to come to grips with just such social and moral issues. According to Haacke, co-optation occurs when the intentions with which our action is taken are reversed in practice, and one ends up serving the opposing interests. The problem is that in spite of all these distortions, museums and galleries as the established channels of communication remain the most powerful tools for getting a message out. So that even artists like Haacke, who remain dedicated to preserving an attitude of skepticism and a critical distance from the system, realize the impossibility of entirely rejecting the moral and social codes of our time. "I'm afraid," Haacke states, "that to forgo the use of these amplifying transmitters for the sake of purity would force me, embittered, into a sectarian corner and in the end would leave me totally impotent. . . . In order to contribute to the gradual decomposition of the belief structure of today's fantastically resilient capitalism, one cannot but mimic and play along with some of its ways. Only history will tell in retrospect who was co-opting whom, if one can really speak of co-optation in such a dialectically complex setting."

In such a setting, one thing is sure: any artist in contemporary society who sets out to create values must engage actively with the outside world—keeping free of the system is no longer a viable option. Solitude paralyzes the faculties, and purity and innocence will only be a handicap. At this point, our whole culture resembles the fly who cannot get through a pane of glass. It is more and more difficult to find a position of estrangement that continues to be relevant, or potent. The negation in the outsider's position has lost its urgency; meanwhile, we find ourselves lodged in a network of proscribed solutions for our lives that commits us to the culture of bureaucracy even while our art rages against it. Since anyone who resists can only survive by joining hands with everything he once rejected, the choice would almost seem to be between artistic or moral suicide. When we candidly examine the value-scales that have been set up, what we are driven to understand is surely the lesson of this age: that art cannot survive along the capitalist "faultline" except by being compromised.

CHAPTER FOUR:
BUREAUCRATIZATION
The Death of the Avant-Garde

For some time now it has been evident that the critical intransigence of the avant-garde is evaporating in front of our eyes. Provocations that once seemed radical have long since lost their power to shock. Even the most difficult art has become comfortably familiar, and the unpredictable predictable. Whether in spite of itself or due to circumstances beyond its control, the vanguard concept has been traded in for good marketing strategy, and has become a big, booming juggernaut. The critic Peter Schjeldahl put it well when he wrote that the ritual anticommercialism of the late '60s and '70s has had "roughly the impact on capitalism of a beanbag hurled against cement."

Those who are concerned over the bankruptcy of modernism frequently argue as though it were a relief to have it over and done with. But the truth is that in many ways the subversive impulse of modernism has been our culture's saving grace; the avant-garde functioned as the conscience of bourgeois civilization, the only antitoxin generated within the body of our society to counteract the pernicious spread of secular, bureaucratic consciousness. I think we shall perhaps only perceive the true meaning of what we have lost by becoming conscious of the dynamics by which modernist culture has been displaced, and of the consequences now posed to the balance of forces within our social scene.

If the adversary psychology of modernism originated in the contradiction between a society with corporate values and interests and the kind of spiritual consciousness that can only come from religion and art, what the death of modernism really signifies is that our art no longer sustains and protects this contradiction. The steady displacement of radical consciousness by the forces of professionalism, bureacracy, and commercialism has caused avant-garde art to lose its power of rebellion and has crippled its impact. Art no longer presents a significant alternative to bourgeois values. In this new situation, what was once seen to be a defect is now raised to a virtue: submission to the established order. Those archetypes of the artist and the businessman, which previously straddled our culture as adversaries, have now joined hands. "Being good in business," writes Andy Warhol, "is the most fascinating kind of art. Making money is art and working is art and good business is the best art. . . . I like money on the wall. Say you were going to buy a $200,000 painting. I think you should take that money, tie it up, and hang it on the wall. Then when someone visited you the first thing they would see is the money on the wall."

Comments like these may be just talk—like everything Warhol does, they are amusing and morally ambiguous, but they leave nobody flinching nowadays; rather, they are a disconcerting sign of just how far artists have drifted in the direction of cultural conformity. Perhaps the most interesting thing about Warhol is the way he brings into question the whole sphere of authenticity. Are his statements ironical, or are they a put-on? Or is he serious? From whatever angle we look at these comments, they manage to preserve their enigmatic character. Warhol guards his secret well— we will never really know what goes on behind the mask. That is the root of his power. But the lack of moral tone of his vision is, at this point, an essential element in the conclusion of the modernist story. Trapped more and more in a situation that seems both hopeless and inescapable, artists have become increasingly dependent on the complicated bureaucratic machinery which now organizes and administers the consumption of art in our culture. This apparatus does much more than merely organize and administer, however; it also preconditions the drives and ambitions of those whose well-being it ostensibly exists to promote. It encourages accommodation and surrender to our society's predominant values, and in so doing, it has undermined the very basis of artistic alienation. The "alienated" element, which, according to Marcuse, was the token of the artist's truth, is now viewed condescendingly. Negativity and opposition have been transformed into acceptance and collusion.

Anyone who doubts the extent to which society's corporate and bureaucratic interests have become the innermost drives of its artists need only consider the number of artists who parachute down in Soho each week, hoping to make it in New York, even if it means hanging from the lampposts until they can secure those emblems of success, a loft and a dealer. Others have commented on Soho's quasi-factory conditions, its atmosphere of mass production, and its daily invasions of trained "modern artists" for whom there are no "jobs" in relation to the market. Recent estimates given for the number of artists in New York begin with 30,000 and go as high as 90,000. The Soho dealer Ivan Karp has commented that he sees up to one hundred artists each week, some ninety percent of whom he considers totally professional, all looking for galleries in which to sell their work.

This has never happened in the past. Such standardization is an example of what Erich Fromm has called "consensual validation"—the assumption that since a majority of people share certain attitudes and feelings, the validity of those attitudes and feelings is proven. But individuality loses its quality of freedom if it is exercised en masse. This social pattern—in which everybody believes that what the majority wants must be worth striving for—now constitutes reality for most artists. Most people seem to accept that this is the way things are. This sharing of a specific social construct of reality among so many members of a given culture gives it the semblance of *natural* reality; the individual responds to this socially constructed reality as if it were constant and not socially conditioned—thus a way of life is established as lawful for all.

When a society is profoundly wrong for the artist, he cannot, after all, remain unaffected. The mental and moral capitulation of our society has no parallel in history. Its effects have invaded everyone's mind and character, so that most of our allegedly radical artists now reflect the culture of consumerism more than they challenge it. "I sure wish," writes California artist and critic Peter Plagens, "I had the balls to be dyspeptically weird, to hate things out loud, to take crazy, half-baked, unprincipled, vacillating stands on pointless questions, to pee in somebody's fireplace. But, Your Honor, I'd also like to become a licensed manufacturer of baubles-for-the-rich, with a palatial studio and a baronial wine cellar. I want Zuni baskets on plexi coffee tables. . . ." That everyone now has like-minded interests precludes the emergence of any effective opposition against the whole system.

Marcuse is very instructive here, pointing out exactly how the productive apparatus becomes totalitarian: how it determines not only social occupations and attitudes, but also individual needs and aspirations. The transformation from rugged individualism into bureaucratic conformism has been induced gradually by a system of economic rewards. Production for profit (whether it is art or consumer goods) is a basic institution of our society; but it has been internalized into a set of needs which the individual now feels he is entitled to satisfy. The painter Robert Henri's comment, made in 1923, only sixty years ago, that "the only sensible way to regard the art life is that it is a privilege you are willing to pay for" is a statement unlikely to have, at this point for our society, any emotive potential whatsoever. The shoe has moved to the other foot—artists now want art to serve their careers rather than seeing themselves as serving art. Creative humility is no longer in style, and it may be worth asking ourselves how such a reversal in our thinking has come about. What was formerly an ideal has become the very framework of ambition: "making it on sales alone." Today, this is quite simply the main measure of an artist's success. "Cash," interpolates Warhol. "I just am not happy when I don't have it. The minute I have it I have to spend it. And I just buy stupid things."

Our culture is perhaps the first completely secularized culture in history, and what seems most ominous at this point is that the whole idea of the artistic vocation—of the artist who renounces worldly ambitions in order to dedicate himself to values that cannot possibly be realized by a commercial society—does not exert much power of attraction any more. Careers depend more and more on advertising, promotion, and good public relations. I'm not saying this is the case for everyone, but that the rationale of success virtually requires this pattern of behavior. We are not likely to see another Albert Pinkham Ryder, a lonely, reclusive artist who lived one hundred years ago and cared nothing for money, social prestige, or comforts. Ryder lived frugally on thirteen cents a day and slept in a carpet roll; at night he wandered the bridges, ferries, and waterfronts of New York, "soaking up the moonlight" and watching the shadows a boat's sail made upon the water. "The artist," Ryder wrote, "must live to paint and not paint to live. He should not sacrifice his ideals to a landlord and a costly studio. A rain-tight roof, frugal living, a box of colors and God's sunlight through clear windows keep the soul attuned and the body vigorous for one's daily work." His refusal of a dealer's offer to pay him liberally for ten pictures to be completed over a period of three years—although he badly needed the money—seems all but unthinkable now, a self-imposed austerity that is mildly eccentric and certainly out-of-date. These are not ideas that today's art major is likely to pick up about his or her role. He or she will learn instead that all serious artists must eventually go to New York. If artists like Ryder were ever role models in the past, they certainly are not today. As it happens, Ryder was somewhat retarded when it came to financial matters, which seemed a complete mystery to him. Checks or cash that came his way were left lying around his rooms, and once, when a fellow artist, Horatio Walker, asked him if he had any money, Ryder replied that "there was some on a paper in the cupboard." Walker then explained about cashing checks, took him to a bank, and helped him open an account. Later Ryder was to describe Walker as not only a fine painter but also a great financier.

Modes and categories inherited from the past no longer seem to fit the social reality experienced by the new genera-tion, for whom the only reliable machinery for making reputations is the bureaucratic art world. New artists know no other standard by which to evaluate things. Social condi-tions today foster a survival mentality—what is admired is an ability to hold one's own and to get ahead. The ways in which Ryder suffered, his religious asceticism, his ardent ideals about art, have all but lost their allure for an art world transformed beyond recognition by material prosperity. Thus, the Pop artist Robert Indiana candidly replied to Bar-baralee Diamonstein, when she asked him in an interview how important it was to be part of the art establishment: "Enormously important, if you want to 'make it.' Everything in life seems to be who you know and when you know them and where you are, and to be in the right place at the right time with the right thing is about what Pop amounted to. And it's certainly my case. . . ." Obviously, skepticism about the rules of the game is not really possible if one wishes to fulfill certain ambitions.

The Australian-born sculptor Clement Meadmore lamented, in an interview with Geoffrey De Groen published in 1981 in *Art and Australia,* his own failure to be in the right place at the right time: "One of the things about American art is that you have to be part of a movement to become well known. If I'd shown the things I did in 1964, if I'd had a gallery by then, I should have been considered one of the Minimalists. It was fairly Minimal work. It wasn't truly Minimal, philosophically, but it would have been near enough to have been lumped in with them, in terms of reviews and writing about it. . . . That didn't happen. . . . [My work] didn't fit into any movement and I never got written about in terms of movements. It's a very slow process then to get known all by yourself. I really should have come here about 1960 and got a gallery, so that by the time I was doing the Minimal works I should have been part of that bandwagon."

Success and security now play such a central role in the American imagination, the inducements of a conformist society are proving so great, that even artists have learned to strive along an imposed scale of careerist values, mapping out their lives like military strategists. If early capitalism led to the formation of ascetic tendencies, late capitalism has spawned a more acquisitive and exploitative form of individualism, together with an art more oriented toward production and profit. Anyone who professes to be motivated by sacrifice or asceticism—by a need to hold something of himself forever from the world's reach—is met by derisive disbelief. Thus it is that modernism's former historic role of rebellion has changed into eager acquiescence in the impulse to advance and become established. It is as if, in the words of Abraham Maslow, the frustrated will to meaning has been compensated by the will to power plus what one might call a "will to money." And once harnessed into the bureaucratic apparatus, the artist becomes chained to his activity as a "producer." He becomes yet another functionary integrated into the mechanism with a vested interest in

70

seeing that the mechanism continues its function. These days art is a "worldly" calling, and the intellectual refusal to go along—to play the game by the rules even if one is lacking in conviction—appears neurotic and impotent.

Such is the tenor of the times that Ryder's exemplary life, his commitment to negotiating on his own terms, doesn't stand for much. For by now, the iconoclastic posture of the artist as an outcast—who stands for another way of life than the established one—whose purpose as a religious, spiritual, or moral hero is to create a symbolic life that will have meaning for others—has been reduced to the same kind of mechanical order and bureaucratic fixity that engulfs other professions in our society. "Why do people think artists are special?" asks Warhol. "It's just another job." This assimilation of creative ideals into an impersonal, calculating, secular reality indicates the extent to which the realm of the soul or spirit has been translated by our material culture into pragmatic terms. Hence the need for endless compromises, and the conflicts arising from the fact that aims and standards have been confused beyond anyone's comprehension.

Obviously, this shift in gears has not been accepted by everyone with equanimity. Undoubtedly the Minimal artist Robert Mangold was speaking for many others when he voiced his disillusionment with the current scene in a recent issue of *Art in America:*

> The early 60s in New York were like the 50s in a sense. It was a very small art scene. You could throw a loft party and literally everybody in the art world would be there. Everything would open on Tuesday evening. In one evening you could see everything that was shown. That changed somewhere around the mid-60s—the size of the art world, the number of galleries, a lot of things started shifting; things also shifted politically. By the end of the 60s the whole scene was very different. I left New York, very disillusioned, in 1970. For one thing, I felt there was a kind of commercialism taking place that I found offensive. I felt the need to put distance between me and the art world. Things were happening that somehow seemed so divisive, and everyone was jealous of everyone else. . . . I just wanted to get the art world out of my head. I didn't want to think about who was on the cover of the art magazines,

or whether this or that article was mentioning me or not. To me it seemed a deadly context to live in.

As we move into the era of postmodernism, we seem to be witnessing the rise of a new psychological type of artist: the bureaucratic or organizational personality who lives in a condition of submission to a cultural and economic power system because of the rewards of money and prestige which are offered in return for such submission. In America, this process is now far advanced as a new power elite of managers continues to grow and consolidate, encompassing all aspects of life. Thomas Whiteside has written eloquently in *The New Yorker* about the corporate takeover of the publishing industry; the same tendencies now threaten all levels of the art world, where a commercial morality can only have the same effect on art as it has had on book publishing: the promotion of mediocre work through aggressive forms of mass-marketing and advertising. The high period of modernism is over, and we are clearly moving on to something else—to the emergence of a new value system, described by William Scott and David Hart in their book *Organizational America* as the "organizational imperative." Scott and Hart believe that the most significant source of the subversion of the individual is the modern organization—in which the moral burdens of autonomy are traded in for the comforts of security. The "organizational imperative" functions on the basis of the idea that whatever is good for the individual can come only from the modern organization. In the case of the art world, the bureaucratic power structure is turned into a quasi-animate personality from whom everything is expected. Bureaucratic rules and procedures take the place of personal morality: this is what institutionalized individuality means. The old values of individuality, indispensability, and spontaneity are replaced by new ones, based on obedience, dispensability, specialization, planning, and paternalism. The goal is security: to be part of the big powerful machine, to be protected by it, and to feel strong in the symbiotic connection with it. In the case of artists, these values are hostile to all that we know about the nature of creativity. And yet, to survive in this new order of things *all* must conform to the requirements of the modern organization—therein lies the problem.

Coincident with this change in mentality are basic, if

hardly acknowledged, changes in the ideas by which life is interpreted. Contemporary American cultural identity now includes the idea that the individual artist cannot function without the aid and guidance of some dealer, an idea which may seem incongruous in a society constantly proclaiming the value of freedom and the independence of the artist. Under the "organizational imperative," what rises to the top through the engineering of taste by media promotion and dealer advertising must be seen to be the best. "To be successful as an artist," according to Warhol, "you have to have your work shown in a good gallery for the same reason that, say, Dior never sold his originals from a counter in Woolworth's. A good gallery looks out for the artist, promotes him and sees to it that his work is shown in the right way to the right people. No matter how good you are, if you're not promoted right you won't be one of those remembered names." Increasing reliance is now placed upon a managerial elite of dealers and curators—who are not only the main means for the promotion of art, even more than critics, but who exercise fairly unassailable control over which art gets promoted—with the result that individuals now exist for the benefit of the organization, rather than the organization for the individual. If they choose to, dealers can ignore artists' demands because they realize that at this point, with a handful of exceptions, artists need dealers even more than dealers need artists. Of course, there will always be some cases that do not fit this state of affairs— but as a basic trend it is still incredible in its stark and simple truth. The following comments by the Soho dealer Ivan Karp, made to Barbaralee Diamonstein, make pretty explicit this inversion of priorities: "We put on forty-four separate exhibits a season, which is more than any art institution in the country. . . . I play an active role with my artists. . . . I am frequently with them and visit their studios. I help them sort out their works. I pronounce opinions and convictions. They don't have to listen to me, but I will only show the works that I like in the gallery. In other words, if an artist who is scheduled to show does not produce the kind of works that I want to dignify my gallery with, then I won't show them."

Like Karp, most dealers—if not all—have long since recognized and learned to exploit a situation in which very little of importance can be accomplished any more outside their organizations. The individual artist in this new scheme of things really is of diminishing importance, and his personal influence more negligible, as he becomes an interchangeable unit among dealers. Like many scientists today, managers tend to be judged, not by the morality of their ends, but by the effectiveness of their means. The dealer Mary Boone, for instance, who at thirty has been described by the media as the "new priestess of the art world," monitors very carefully all the sales of her artists' works. One cannot just arrive off the street and buy a Julian Schnabel, no matter what one's resources are. Boone's shows are frequently sold out before they open, but she does not sell to "just anyone." Collectors are carefully screened according to how influential they are, and how frequently they buy from the gallery. Replying to the accusation that she orchestrates her artists' careers, Boone commented in *Life:* "If an artist is introduced and doesn't make the right splash, he may never recover . . . not enough can be said of the importance of developing an entire image for the artists I represent: placing the painter in certain shows, getting the right attention from the right art magazines, throwing the right parties at the right clubs. It's all so very important." Janelle Reiring, co-director of the Metro Pictures Gallery in Soho, speaks for many of the younger, new, successful dealers when she claims that being a dealer today "is not the pursuit of a nineteenth-century gentleman. Business is one of its most interesting aspects, and I think you will be seeing more —and more aggressive—dealers."

Clearly, all this has not happened suddenly. But as the difficulty of climbing out of the current becomes greater and greater, artists—for the sake of their careers—must increasingly shut their eyes to the hopelessness of ever harmonizing their aspirations, standards, and ambitions with the economic and social demands of the times. Since there is little doubt at this point that the career progress of professionals depends on making organizational values an intrinsic part of their lives, the artist gears his aspirations and his work to the situation he is in, and from which he can find no way out. Many artists remain prickly and ambivalent about this state of affairs, but the pressure to conform usually supersedes the importance of trying to achieve consistency between one's beliefs and actions. As the young Italian Neo-expressionist Sandro Chia remarked on the occasion of his inclusion in the last international art exhibition "Documenta" held in Kassel, Germany: "I feel it was both coarse and superficial to invite someone like me to take part, when I am one of the first to hope that their undertaking will be a failure." And so it is that everything that is done today—even in one's inner conscience—is provisional. Ultimately, the problem of real moral choice must be shunted aside by anyone keen on status advance.

Hegel never said that the direction taken by history was "ineluctably necessary," but only that history can be seen to have happened as he described it. The truth is that modern managerial practices, which have come more and more to set the tone of our society and to establish its cultural pace, were not central to the attitudes of such early art dealers as Alfred Stieglitz and Henry Kahnweiler. Stieglitz, who established the first American gallery devoted to avant-garde art in New York, found it necessary to sacrifice the practice of his own photography in order to nurture the creative development of the artists—Arthur Dove, Marsden Hartley, John Marin, and Georgia O'Keeffe—whom he believed in. He did not charge a standard commission, and the gallery lost money; but Stieglitz was not looking to reach a large audience or to become famous himself. When he first opened the Secession Gallery in 1905 (it was later to become Gallery 291), there was no publicity. "Those who love and understand and have the art-nose will find their way," he said. One of his artists, Marie Rapp, has described how Stieglitz had no time for those who saw art in financial terms or who bought for investment: "What he resented more than anything else was to have someone who had money come in and offer to buy a painting as if it were a shop or as if the work were some commodity. If he thought they wanted to buy just because they had money, he might double the price of the painting. If someone else came in and was just crazy about something, and had nothing else in mind, he would let them have it for half-price!"

The extent to which "unworldly" values have fallen from grace in our own times is nowhere more grimly exemplified than in the conspiracy to defraud the Rothko estate after the artist's death, which was instigated by his dealer Frank Lloyd, the director of a multimillion-dollar international network of Marlborough galleries. The climax of this affair was a criminal lawsuit in 1972 that dragged on for months and months, through nineteen lawyers and 20,000 pages of testimony, and was described at the time in *New York* magazine as "the art world's own little Watergate."

Henry Kahnweiler, by contrast, was as dedicated in his approach to art as was Stieglitz. When Kahnweiler launched the first "modernist" pictures of Picasso and Braque in his gallery in the rue Vignon in 1907, he categorically refused to exhibit them in the public salons. Like Stieglitz, Kahnweiler kept healthy little daggers of contempt up his sleeve for what he considered the merchandising approach, and for the mass consumption of art. "People always think that an art dealer 'launches' painters with a lot of fanfare or publicity," he writes in his memoirs. "I didn't spend a cent, not even for announcements in the paper. . . . In the old days, people went to the Indépendents to get mad or to laugh. In front of certain pictures, there would be groups of people writhing with laughter or howling with rage. We had no desire to expose ourselves either to their rage or to their laughter, so we stopped showing the pictures." Protected from the need to play to large audiences by their dealer, Picasso and Braque were able to pursue Cubism as a private and personal exploration. Seventy years later, in 1980, more than a million people visited the Picasso retrospective at the Museum of Modern Art in New York. The show cost $2½ million to put together, and seven thousand people a day came and went. Many of them had to purchase tickets in advance, and the overwhelming floods of visitors meant that 105 attendants had to stand guard over the pictures at all times.

Changes in the marketing of art are by no means limited to the private sector of commercial dealers, however: mutant intentions have also redefined and altered the role of the museum. As government endowments and private funds diminish and operating costs increase, many museums have turned to corporations for support. Over the past decade many large corporations, most notably oil companies, have gained a considerable foothold in U.S. museums. In New York, for instance, few major exhibitions are produced any more without corporate money. Contributions to the arts from corporate philanthropy in America has risen from $23 million in 1963 to $463 million in 1979. Supporting the arts provides corporate sponsors with an opportunity to enhance their public image. The artist Hans

Haacke, who has published articles, given interviews, and made art exposing the corporate rationale for the support of art, has described how, during the 1960s, the more sophisticated executives of large corporations began to understand that the association of their company's name with the arts could have considerable long-term benefits. Under the seeming altruism of underwriting museum exhibitions, cultural television programs, or concerts, a large oil or cigarette company with a public-relations problem realized that by associating its name with a human activity that carries high social prestige, it could improve the company image. One Mobil public-relations man, for instance, has described the payoff his company receives for its tax-deductible contribution to culture as its "goodwill umbrella."

Haacke frequently uses his own art to provoke a critical consciousness about this situation. One of his works involved collecting a series of statements (mostly found in management journals) made by corporate executives and politicians as to the good business rationale of supporting the arts. Haacke reproduced these statements on aluminum plaques in a style imitating the technique of corporate advertising. One statement, for instance, had been made by David Rockefeller, as Chairman of Chase Manhattan Bank and Vice Chairman of the Museum of Modern Art, in a speech to the National Industrial Conference Board. It reads: "From an economic standpoint, such involvement [in the arts] can mean direct and tangible benefits. It can provide a company with extensive publicity and advertising, a brighter public reputation, and an improved corporate image. It can build better customer relations, a readier acceptance of company products, and a superior appraisal of their quality. Promotion of the arts can improve the morale of employees and help attract qualified personnel."

Corporations are inevitably interested in sponsoring exhibitions that are likely to yield the greatest public-relations dividends through their popular and sensational appeal. Throughout the organization of the show, and particularly in its promotion, the corporate influence is felt. Exhibitions themselves will often become "merchandise" and the public a "market." When the Tutankhamen exhibition was held at the Metropolitan Museum ("the sort of thing any corporation would love to support," according to Thomas Messer, Director of the Guggenheim Museum), it was accompanied by bulk merchandising on such a scale that for months "King Tut" became a trademark image. The New York critic Carter Ratcliff commented at the time in *Art in America:* "For the Tut glut to qualify as a full-scale cultural phonomenon, there has to be a link between the consumption of mass-experience and the consumption of mass-produced products." A great deal of businesslike attention was given over to enticing the public to buy Tut T-shirts, bath towels, silk scarves, rock-and-roll records, tie clasps, tote bags, and calendars. It is one of the paradoxes of our present society that the more art becomes an available commodity, the less it becomes a rare treasure. As the links between business and art proliferate, the atmosphere of museums has changed in quality and tone. Under the new cultural style, the success of an exhibition is measured—in Hollywood terms—by media coverage and box office. Attendance figures become the great yardstick for everything.

Since museums first stumbled onto the road of corporate image-building, the addiction to corporate funds has steadily grown. Today, the managerial elite is winning everywhere; its power is such that it has re-formed the expectations we have for our lives, and reordered our priorities. As organization and management penetrate further into the social order, there is no longer much difference between what artists define as their individual aims and what managers try to accomplish within their organizations. The bureaucrat's main desire is to advance, and he can best do so by becoming part of the organizational imperative. Another telling example of how much career progress, even in art, now depends on making organizational values an intrinsic part of one's life may be seen in the "Survival Workshop" that took place during the summer of 1981 at the University of Maryland. These workshops are now proliferating. The assumption is that success in the higher corporate world of art requires training in the techniques of business administration, and it leaves no doubt that the principles and practices of corporate management now produce the psychological model shaping even the lives of artists.

It is not so much that the defects of bureaucracy and commercialism have begun to outweigh their virtues, but that everyone, including artists, now reinforce the same values. All these tendencies toward conformism merely help to endorse the assumption that the avant-garde, and its

MARYLAND SUMMER INSTITUTE
For the Creative and Performing Arts
and
U.S. SMALL BUSINESS ADMINISTRATION

in cooperation with
National Endowment for the Arts
National Assembly of State Arts Agencies
Artists Equity Association, Inc.
University of Maryland Department of Art

present

THE BUSINESS OF
A·R·T
AND THE
A·R·T·I·S·T

Survival Workshop for the 80's
Monday-Friday, June 8-12, 1981
UNIVERSITY OF MARYLAND
COLLEGE PARK

THE PROFESSIONAL ARTIST   June 8
Balancing Your Life • Alternative Careers • Goal Setting • Designing
Your Living/Work Space • Assertiveness Training • Health Hazards

BUSINESS AND LAW   June 9
Contracts • Copyrights/Patents/Trademarks • Co-operatives • Non-Profit
Organizations • Estate Planning/Retirement/Insurance •
Budgeting/Accounting/Record Keeping/Taxes

THE MARKETPLACE   June 10
Galleries/Collectors • Museums • Corporations • Commissions •
Alternative Art Spaces

THE ART OF MARKETING   June 11
Photographing Your Work • Portfolios/Resumes • Pricing •
Packaging/Display/Shipping • Promotion/Agents

GRANTS AND SERVICES   June 12
National Endowment for the Arts • U.S. Small Business Administration
State Arts Councils • Foundations • Slide Repositories/Registries

REGISTRATION is open to the general public. Workshop fee is $15.00 per day or $50.00 for all 5 days. Space is limited. Early registration recommended. The University of Maryland, College Park Campus is nine miles northeast of downtown Washington D.C. On-Campus accommodations available at reasonable rates.

For information, brochure and application call (301) 454-5910 or 454-2763, or write MSICPA, Summer Programs, University of Maryland, College Park, MD 20742.

79

modes of protest and resistance, have become obsolete or irrelevant. Whatever complex crosscurrents are still to be found in the present art scene, the dominant tendency does seem to be adjustment to the system, and capitulation to its major agencies of control. To dwell on the dark side of this, however, is to blaspheme against our religion of prosperity and success. But the notion of art as a counterforce is no longer being defended—the critical obligation to dissidence has lost its hold on the moral imagination. And yet, as Irving Howe noted already in 1962, the future of any worthwhile modern culture would seem to depend precisely on the survival of the kind of dedicated group that the avant-garde has been. The need for refusal and subversion is, if anything, even more urgent now than it was fifty years ago, before the corporate elements of our society began to distort beyond recognition the inner life of the world in which art is produced. Certainly there is nothing at this point that gives us cause for reassurance or relaxation—nothing that gives us reason to turn our backs on principled dissent.

The growing acquiescence in the aims and practices of bureaucratic society troubles many observers of modern culture. Corporate bureaucracies have as their avowed mission the production and sale of goods and services at a profit; they are chiefly institutions for selling and marketing. Values alien to the efficiency of operation are abolished. The self-determined, independent, creative being becomes just another cog in the mechanism which prescribes to him a fixed route of march. It was Max Weber's greatest fear toward the end of his life that the world might one day be filled with nothing but these little cogs, little men clinging to little jobs and striving toward bigger ones; he wondered how to keep a portion of mankind free from "this parceling-out of the soul," as he put it, from this supreme mastery of the bureaucratic way of life.

Until now, that oppositional force in our society has been embodied in the small, conscious elite known as the avant-garde, and in its permanent challenge to the established order. Being an artist has always meant maintaining a certain independence of mind and not adapting to the competitive performances required for well-being under the established system, even at the cost of intense personal sacrifice. But since Ryder's time, we have experienced a radical decline in the individual's potential to stand firm and alone. There seems to be nothing innate in individuals that will force them to resist if the rewards for adaptation are sufficient. There is no reason to insist on self-determination, as Marcuse has shown, if the administered life is comfortable; the need for refusal is arrested by our society's "delivering the goods" on a huge scale. After all, if everyone is happy with the rewards handed down by the system, why should anyone demand that things be different? Affluence is the great social tranquilizer.

But as the years go by, all these benefits and rewards exert a hidden pressure, and the temptation to strike out on one's own, or to take another path, becomes less and less. What is more, every act of compliance constitutes positive feedback—a vote of confidence for the system. The problem has never been as acute as it is today, because individual conscience has never before been replaced by an organizational imperative that relieves one of the task of thinking for oneself. In accepting its reality, we are becoming all the same, as our allegiance quietly shifts from individualism to obedience in following the same managerial rules and goals. Accepting our society's stress on achievement and economic growth has provoked a crisis for artists, distorting the ways in which they value art and altering their motives for creating it. How is it possible, then, for artists living in a society centered on production, consumption, and success to become independent personalities once again, and to once more exert their influence on society? Only, perhaps, by the willingness to apply an inner brake that says "no" to the dominant claims of our times, even when everybody else says "yes." Rather than vainly attempting to abolish the system, it will mean altering the values that motivate one's striving. Marcuse also makes the point that unless revolt reaches into this "second" nature—that is to say, into the infrastructure of our longings and needs—social change will remain self-defeating. The future prospects of art obviously depend very much on how artists define their needs and aspirations, and how they interpret their own interests.

One thing, anyway, is clear. If present trends continue, we are almost certain to wind up in circumstances whose long-range implications for the future of art are negative. "Management" is a recent phenomenon, not more than seventy-five years old. As Scott and Hart emphasize, it is dominant because we made it so. "We did this," they state, "because we believed that the modern organization would provide us with material affluence, physical safety and peace of mind. We were not aware . . . that we would have to buy a whole sack full of new values in the process. But something does not come for nothing; once the organizational imperative was set in motion, it became so powerful that we lost our sense of how to control it, let alone how to turn it off." As a society, we have become so hooked on environmental and bureaucratic artificiality that there seems little chance of escape from it. The agonies of even partial withdrawal are more than most of us dare contemplate. It must be said, however, that at this point the machine can be controlled only by people willing to change their whole value system, their whole world view, and their whole way of life.

CHAPTER FIVE: PLURALISM
The Tyranny of Freedom

Postmodernism is the somewhat weasel word now being used to describe the garbled situation of art in the '80s. It is a term which nobody quite fully understands, because no clear-cut definition of it has yet been put forward. Its use arose synonymously with that of pluralism toward the end of the '70s, and at that point it referred to the loss of faith in a stylistic mainstream, as if the whole history of styles had suddenly come unstuck. Since then, under the more recent umbrella of Neo-expressionism, the old stylistic divisions now mix, blend, and alternate interchangeably with each other: dogmatism and exclusivity have given way to openness and coexistence. Pluralism abolishes controls; it gives the impression that everything is permitted. Meeting with no limitation, the artist is free to express himself in whatever way he wishes.

If modernism was ideological at heart—full of strenuous dictates about what art could, and could not, be—postmodernism is much more eclectic, able to assimilate, and even plunder, all forms of style and genre and circumstance, and tolerant of multiplicity and conflicting values. Originally, the modernist assertion of self represented a rebellion: by taking a path of active, self-sacrificing struggle, modern artists sought to improve the ethical image of our world. Central to avant-gardism were the concept of alienation and

83

protest and the assumption that art must be something more than the production of superfluous luxury products. The *engagement* of modernism, even in its most "alienated" manifestations of art for art's sake or anti-art, always involved a negative attitude toward bourgeois society: refusal of easy success, dissatisfaction with the values of the marketplace, and that permanent revolution waged against the tempting habit of conformity. One of the things that seems to separate postmodernist from modernist thinking—and the one that will concern me particularly here—is the rejection of any serious concern about art's moral center. "There is a morality of art," the composer Arnold Schönberg observed in the heroic early days of modernism, "to serve as a counterpart to this world that is in many respects giving itself up to amoral, success-ridden materialism in the face of which all the ethical preconditions of our art are steadily disappearing."

That comment was made at a time when modernist culture was uncompromisingly dissident and subversive—when its current was still running very much against the tidal patterns of the larger culture. Now, of course, there is a decidedly open alliance between society as a whole and art's economic status, and once-"alienated" works have acquired an investment value beyond anybody's imagining. The result is a currently thriving art industry, in which the artist has become the means for the economic interest of other people, or himself, or the economic machine—while the ethical coordinates that give art its tutelary force are being obliterated. Nearly all art today is the product of energies freed from direct social purpose or obligation. What began before World War I as a burning involvement of artists in the future of their societies (this was the radical and evolutionary implication of the term avant-garde) had subsided by the mid-1970s into acknowledgment that art would never change the world. In the era of postmodernism, heroism and high art are out of style.

It was this loss of hope, more than anything else, that transformed the avant-garde from an ethical into an aesthetic movement. Speaking of how the concept of the "sublime" has been increasingly devalued by our skeptical age, and of the "scaled-down ambitions" of our artists, the critic Peter Schjeldahl wrote recently in *Art in America:*

> Art as a substitute religion—and it was no less than this for Rothko, as for Mondrian—has disappointed us, and there is a general understanding, I think, that artistic grandeur is not worth the terrible human investment required to attain it. That's the way things are. It would be more than a shame, however, to let our understandable present cynicism be made retroactive, denigrating great work created at the last high tide of artistic faith . . . for it is the pressure of the values that creates the intensity of the work, and to assume otherwise is to have no comprehension of how art actually happens. . . . Rothko lacked the wisdom of the '70s, which seems to be that to believe in anything at all is messy and dangerous, and this does give us an edge on him.

In many ways, the abandonment of ideology in favor of a pluralist situation seems to offer colossal and unparalleled opportunities for every kind of artistic expression; it would seem, moreover, to be a liberating release from intolerant exclusiveness and from the avant-garde imperative of continual innovation. But there are negative consequences lurking undetected in such an "overoptioned" situation which threaten our art with the imprint of meaninglessness. It is not my intention to inject cynicism or doubt into what many people consider the invigorating effects of so much stylistic freedom, but I do perceive that there are two sides of this emerging tendency that need to be pondered. The positive benefits of pluralism go hand in hand with its negative, or disintegrative, character.

For one thing, allowing unlimited freedom of expression in a sense undermines the importance of what is expressed, while the sheer overavailability of options actually lowers the degree of innovation possible. In the early days of modernism, to experiment was to have the feeling of being poised on some outermost brink; departing from the norm was a radical act that meant staking one's life as an artist and risking everything. In the new pluralistic situation, however, all modes of art can claim equal status, and they do. Many divergent claims to authority have begun by now to undermine and weaken art's integrity and plausibility, since what pluralism really means is that the lines between what is acceptable as art and what is unacceptable no longer exist. Everything can now be accommodated. The problem with the option of accommodation, however, is that once taken, it tends to escalate to the point where the plausibility of the tradition collapses, as it were, from within. The disintegration is not merely of this or that aesthetic assumption, but of the overall pattern of meaning. When the natural order of things runs down, we get entropy—a move from systemic order toward increasing randomness and loss of direction. What I am saying is that once art no longer lays claim to the dignity of the absolute, it loses its charismatic, "meaning-giving" function.

For a tradition to be in place, there have to be some shared standards of excellence, some rules that are already established. These standards and rules cannot be determined by the individual—their authority derives from the fact of being socially determined by the practice. Only then can we criticize and try to change them. The central attitude of pluralism—that art is various, that whatever artists define as art is acceptable as an "end" to be pursued—breaks down the unity of a narrative history that until now has made art intelligible and sustained its practice. Once there is no longer any ultimate agreement as to the rules which constitute and sustain a practice—once there is no longer anything to impose constraints—all that pluralism can do is obscure the depths of our conflicts. Hilton Kramer alluded to the problem some time ago in *The New York Times:*

> If there is something appealing in the very openness of this postmodernist art scene, there is also something dismaying in it, too. For it reminds us that ours is now a culture without a focus or center. . . . Perhaps we know too much about art to believe in the absolute efficacy of any single style or tradition. Are we condemned, then, in the art of the '80s, to remain in a perpetual whirl of countervailing and contradictory styles and attitudes? I think we probably are. This eager embrace of art of every persuasion seems to suit us. It satisfies our hearty new appetite for aesthetic experience while requiring nothing from us in the way of commitment or belief.

Whether we like it or not, traditions have histories; to succeed they need to generate stable and durable criteria. It is possible that what we most need from art at this point is a counterinsistence on psychological stability and on the preservation of certain continuities—or exactly the opposite of what we are getting. Even the "estranged" artist needs to find moral identity in and through a network of social obligations and responsibilities: the notion of escape is an illusion, and one with painful consequences. Pluralism means we can no longer rely on tradition or cultural habit to give us our values. But in such a circumstance, it is possible to become value-blind, like a person who is color-blind or tone-deaf.

Traditional societies have many disadvantages—which include considerable restraints on freedom—but as we find it harder and harder to resolve our own dilemmas, we may come to see the logic of traditional systems with new eyes. We may begin to perceive that it is wrongheaded—and perhaps even fatal—to have no proven standards of value, no constitutive rules that are inviolate. The extreme degree of freedom offered by our present-day pluralism has placed everyone under increased pressure to choose for themselves among unlimited alternatives. But with the breakdown of social consensus, it has become harder and harder to know how or what to choose, or how to defend or validate one's choice. The freedom from all determinants leads to an indeterminacy so total that, finally, one has no reason for choosing anything at all. Pluralism is the norm which cancels all norms. It means we no longer know where the truth lies. (The only truth pluralism allows is that it is absolutely true there is no such thing as absolute truth.) But if values no longer admit of truth and are merely arbitrary, if art is something always provisional and never definitive, how shall we ever grasp its meaning? For either we accept that there are real and inherent values—eternal truths which transcend individual existence—or there are no such truths, in which case we are free to make them up, and one meaning is as good as another. But if all ideas are equal, what can vouchsafe to art its charismatic power and its moral authority? Arbitrariness is the pitfall of unlimited freedom. How can meaning survive when nothing acts as a regulating principle within the practice to protect whatever presuppositions and interests are involved?

We have come full circle from traditional society where the individual was rarely, if ever, thrown back on himself. Not only are our artists at liberty to make art in any manner they please, they must choose between alternatives whether they like it or not. As Peter Berger has pointed out, "Modern consciousness entails a movement from fate to choice." Choice is a modern idea; there was no choice in traditional societies. Our relativistic philosophy may seem more appealing, but it has against it the deeper instinct that too much freedom has distinctly negative consequences for the emotional economy of the individual. The "anguish of choice," which has been written about so eloquently by Erich Fromm, can become a burden and a danger, since everything now depends on the individual's own effort, and not on the security of his traditional status. Whatever certainty there is must be dredged up from within the subjective consciousness of the individual; it can no longer be derived from the external, socially shared world of meanings and values. In taking away our faith in transcendence, and our respect for authority, modernity has made us all fearful about belief in anything. It has also made us isolated and anxious, and denied us the certainty of being part of some larger purpose. We take the absence of superior forces to be liberating, preferring autonomy; but the cost of such freedom has been the loss of security that comes from tradition and which would normally guarantee for art both moral and practical significance. Indeed, according to Fromm, insecurity is what ultimately breeds the compensatory craving for fame and the compulsive striving for success. Fromm even goes so far as to claim that the character traits engendered by our particular socioeconomic system, and by our way of living, are actually pathogenic. Because the circumstances which surround modern man diminish him and damage him psychically, they eventually produce a sick person and a sick society.

It can be argued, of course, that ever since the Renaissance—a period which saw the transformation of the artist from an anonymous craftsman into an intellectual with special creative powers—artists have always been preoccupied with the pursuit of fame and fortune. Ambition, greed, and self-seeking were not exactly absent from the social structure at that time, a period which saw the rise of desires for recognition and status that were rare or unknown earlier. Vasari's *Lives of the Artists,* for instance, is full of waggish accounts of professional rivalry, such as the jealousy that Torrigiano, a minor artist, felt toward Michelangelo on seeing him much more honored and talented than himself.

Torrigiano began by mocking Michelangelo and at one point hit him on the nose so hard he broke it—for which undignified conduct he got himself banished from Florence. Have things really changed such a great deal since then?

I think the answer is that they have. Individualism took a different form in the past, being tempered by social and aesthetic controls and balanced by a more harmonious development of spiritual powers. The Renaissance was a world in which the sacred and the secular were still united: Leonardo's interest in technology, engineering, and machinery was counterbalanced by an equally lively interest in the world of nature and of the spirit. The difference between earlier conditions and those of today lies in the tension between individualism and communal values, and in the belief or nonbelief in higher realms of being—domains of existence that begin precisely where science stops. Belief is the ontological divide that separates tradition from modernity. In the Renaissance, the artist's mission was twofold: a direct one imposed by the requirements of city, church, or patron, and an indirect one arising from the need to express individuality and to find originality within an established order. A work of art was an individual achievement *and* a social fact, the affirmation of obedience to an established order, and the transcendence, through originality, of that obedience. Although the artist had come to recognize himself as an individual with a free personality—and was no longer satisfied to create anonymously, as in the Middle Ages—he was equally conscious of himself as a social being. In Italy at the time of the Renaissance, Jacob Burckhardt has written, we find artists "who in every branch created new and perfect works, and who also made the greatest impression as men. Others, outside the arts they practised, were masters of a vast circle of spiritual interests." The fifteenth century is, above all, the era of the whole man, known for what the Renaissance called *virtù*—the capacity for showing oneself a man—not the specialist absorbed solely by professional ambitions. Religion provided a source of authority that opposed itself to more worldly pursuits: the individual's dependence on God made just as high a claim on him as the world did. The self had not yet acquired its illusion of self-sufficiency. It had not yet come to believe it had all the rights and none of the social obligations. Individual striving was thus kept in balance because it was but one variable in a total system. Late capitalism, by contrast, has maximized this particular variable to such an extent that it seems to have broken the inward harmony of the social organism as a whole, causing it to go runaway, and maybe even to destroy itself.

Our present situation is one in which art, having abdicated any connection with a transcendental realm of being, has lost its character as a world-view—as a way of interpreting either nature or history. In other societies, the fundamental function of transcendental systems has been the avoidance of chaos and the overcoming of contingency —the very contingency that modernism so self-consciously embraced and raised to a virtue. Such systems provided art with its "meaning-giving" function, and kept it from lapsing into mere self-expression: traditional authority has always drawn its vitality and influence precisely from the belief that its values transcend those of any one individual and go beyond merely personal aims. The modern artist, by contrast, assumes the freedom to express himself as his natural, established condition, without any special cause for it. Nothing from outside incites this freedom to recognize limits to itself or to refer to any authority higher than itself. The pragmatic liberalism of Western society renounces every transcendent goal in favor of freedom and the private enjoyment of life; but if we have gone to great lengths to prove we cannot live with such authority, we have not yet proved that we can live successfully without it. For those who see transcendence as being as vital to the human mind as hope—and as indestructible—the irreverence of modernism is a real threat to the social and psychological bases of human greatness. It may well be that the individual, in order to believe in himself, must believe in the existence of something which surpasses and supports him; and in the same way, it may be that art needs collective ideologies, if only to overcome them from time to time by the force of personality. Society—if not the individual—needs such pillars of truth and authority to guarantee its continuity and permanence. Indeed, the fluctuating relationship between individual freedom and social constraint constitutes, for each society, a field in which it organizes itself—that is why different societies have different moral densities.

What I have been trying (in several ways) to establish is that the more closely we examine the pursuit of freedom in

modern society, the more we come up against an unac-
knowledged split between our ethical and our aesthetic
standpoints. The present system encourages the artist's desire to be thought of as radical and revolutionary; it allows
great freedom of rhetoric, but it does not insist that we
match our lives to the rhetoric. We tend to take this phenomenon for granted, because in our society talent is so
often detached from the personality as a whole and used as
a kind of skilled gadget that can be marketed successfully.
This was nowhere better exemplified than in the way graffiti
artists were suddenly taken up by establishment dealers
after the "Times Square Show" organized by members of
Colab (Collaborative Projects, Inc.) in 1981. It was yet another attempt, by a group of young dissident artists, to
produce "unsalable" art as a specific reaction against the
art-marketing system. Some one hundred artists were included, and despite the studied crudity of the works, the
show received wide media attention, much of it friendly.
Obviously, being approached subsequently by rich galleries
puts the "outsider" artist in a hopeless double-bind, and
requires him to make decisions that are crucial for his future
life—in this case, mostly at an age when few, if any, are
likely to have the strength to carry out what their individual
conscience demands, and what the economic conditions of
the times may make virtually impossible.

It would certainly seem that in order to get back on the
road to *moral* (as distinct from aesthetic) innovation, there
must be some alienation from the current social and economic imperatives that seem so inexorably to condition our
expectations and aspirations. There must be some reintro-
duction of the kinds of ideals that in recent years have fallen
into ruin. If we observe which human achievements attain
the highest honors, we find them always to be those which
manifest the most depth, the most exertion, the most per-
sistent concentration of the whole being; it is a matter of the
individual's struggle in life to make maximum demands on
himself, rather than demanding nothing special of himself.
The trend nowadays is for an ever more one-sided type of
professional achievement which, at its highest point, often
permits the personality as a whole to fall into neglect. Channeling all one's energies into an exclusive task does not leave
much time to renew the life-principle. The assembly-line
mentality that characterizes so much art-making today

causes the artist to lose that necessary contact with the flow of life, and makes his activity become mechanical—a dead formula, emptied of meaning and its original emotional impact. If creativeness lies equally at the root of artistic talent *and* of life experience, the most important object of productiveness will be the human personality itself, which must be perpetually made over. The work of art, then, is merely the evidence of the individual's self-transformation—the tracks, but not the actual animal. Build living Buddhas, says the Zen maxim, not pagodas.

The essence of a personality that has achieved a high degree of growth and integration is that it radiates being-authority. Such people demonstrate by *what they are* as much as by what they do. "My work is writing," William Saroyan once said, "but my real work is being." It is as if all our frantic *doing* has involved a loss of being—as if the tremendous expansion of artistic production has been accompanied by a shrinkage of the individual personality—together with the contents and the significance of life as a whole. To us, productivity means efficiency of output—works of art coming off an ethically blank assembly line like automobiles—but not the individual's potential for creating *himself,* for becoming, as Aristotle proposed, an excellent person. The goal of the *aesthetic* life is one's own satisfaction, whereas casting off conformist ambitions and setting an example of high spiritual devotion is what gives one's mode of life an *ethical* stamp. Certainly, as a culture, we no longer believe in the value of hardship or risk; we no longer take the view that art derives its special quality precisely from the burdens and sacrifices undergone to achieve it. All of the resources of the permissive society are directed toward making things easy, and the capacities for heroism—for courage, sacrifice, and for self-transcendence—are being eradicated, denied by the emergence of a character *that does not want to appear exceptional.*

Generally speaking, the dynamics of professionalization do not dispose artists to accept their moral role; professionals are conditioned to avoid thinking about problems that do not bear directly on their work. They believe the job is what counts in their life—is what gives meaning to their actions. Our radical disenchantment with regard to the artist's "vocation" was made evident during a symposium held at Julian Schnabel's New York loft in the spring of 1982.

Artists Ross Bleckner, Brice Marden, Francesco Clemente, Sandro Chia, Susan Rothenberg, Joel Shapiro, and David Salle were gathered together to show slides and talk about their work before an audience of other art-world luminaries. Afterwards, a question from a member of the audience seemed to embarrass everyone. Did they think, the questioner asked, that their success in the world implied any moral responsibility? "No," said Rothenberg; "we're just folks." David Salle laughed. "That's wrong," said Marden, "we're very unusual people because we're free." Schnabel extended his arms and shrugged. "Of course we have a responsibility to the public. That's why we're here, aren't we?" After which, as one commentator on the scene remarked, everyone shut up. The episode testifies to just how barren is our comprehension at this point of any moral imperative—that is, of any necessary relation between freedom and responsibility. Our culture no longer makes moral demands—on the contrary, it permits us more and more, while demanding of us less and less—so that we have lost the ability to think our way through to the moral foundations of what we are and what we do. Our artists are paid to produce, not to make themselves into exemplary beings.

The notion that an artist or intellectual might actually risk his life in pursuit of an idea—like Solzhenitsyn, who wrote always with the knowledge that a single line could cost him his life—or might undergo the kind of existential suffering that someone like van Gogh did, has become repugnant to a society ruled, fed, and clothed in accordance with the standards of affluence. Material or psychological deprivation has become difficult to grasp, and appears as false heroics—a self-conscious abdication from success and freedom and acceptance of intolerable limitations or sacrifices. Only among Russian dissidents do we still find that kind of struggle and brave refusal—and the kind of moral transcendence that seeks to create values rather than accommodate itself to the existing order. But as André Sakharov has remarked, the fact that Western artists face no threat of prison or labor camp for taking public stands in no way diminishes their responsibility. The struggle to preserve those ethical values—the defense of mankind's lasting interests—is the responsibility of every artist. For only in this can art find its justification, and the creative powers their real depth. One of the chief functions of a cultural tradition is the creation of exemplary models for a whole society, life histories which may be held up as paradigms or archetypes, and which give meaning and create value.

Jackson Pollock once said that every good painter paints what he is. And Duchamp claimed he did not believe in art, but only in artists. What our postmodern age has yet to resolve for itself is its own cultural and social definition of the artist, which may also involve a redefinition of how artists see themselves. Self-images are important: we tend to fashion ourselves to their likenesses, coming to resemble the portraits we draw. Obviously, the governing personality-images that have served Western culture in the past cannot be made consistent with the values of a modern secularized society; the contrast between the past and the present is too enormous. Does truth lie, for instance, in the lonely defiance of van Gogh, bruised by poverty and pain, who claimed that the only lesson we have to learn from life is how to stand up to suffering, or does someone like Warhol provide us with a model image for the artist in our time, with his social bravura and celebrity life, playing it straight to a world in which everyone can be famous for fifteen minutes? (According to Warhol, fame is what makes life livable.) No one is likely to dispute the extent to which these conflicting images of power and personality are totally at odds with each other. They give us two very different images of the destiny and possibilities of being human. It may well be that the notion of the artist as a special individual, as a charismatic figure poised to transcend the cultural categories—an individual who holds nonconformist perceptions of truth that result in conscious and independent moral innovation—has been replaced by a quite different sort of social character, one who prefers to forfeit the charismatic role, and who has scaled down his ambitions to conform to society's idea of the normalized job-holder.

The real test, of course, is not whether an artist subverts social and aesthetic norms in his work, but whether or not his character-structure obeys them: nonconformity in one's work does not necessarily mean nonconformity in character-structure. The writer Murray Kempton once observed in a meditation on the personality of Stefan Cardinal Wyszynski that "the great lives are lived *against* the perceived current of their times. There are men who change history by stubborn resistance to it and they represent the greatness that rises from appreciating the relevance of what the modern mind tends to dismiss as obsolescent. Churchill would have ceased to be Churchill the first moment he decided to be someone more up-to-date than a seventeenth-century Whig; and Wyszynski could not have been Wyszynski if he had ever left off being a thirteenth-century bishop." To be of one's own time, as far as the painter Ingres was concerned, was a measure of failure rather than an achievement.

In a sense, what is really at stake is the relationship between the charismatic and the ordinary. Max Weber has defined charisma as "a certain quality of an individual personality by virtue of which he is set apart from ordinary men and treated as endowed with special qualities." Charismatic figures change the tradition of their societies by their exemplary conduct; as outstanding personalities, they act directly on the conduct of other persons in their own time. Charisma, in Weber's view, was the only conceivable bulwark against the seemingly irresistible force of bureaucratization and the channeling of energies within the confines of a limited and overspecialized task. Obviously, both the romantic and the modern artist accumulated influence by assuming this role—of strong, charismatic persons who seek, on the whole, to put themselves outside the routine ways and assumptions of everyday life, including its comforts and securities; and who, trusting their inner experience, have gone their own individual ways, taking the risks of overt deviation. When we refer to the avant-garde, we are really speaking of just such isolated figures, who have shared the burdens of intransigence and alienation; writers and artists who have been ready to take the consequences of their choices.

Charisma is essentially unstructured power; it is not programmed to advance one's status or to make money—the kind of mental "set" with which so many artists now approach the world, and the view of life that generally propels them into action. At this point, the long-term development of occupational roles, and the emphasis on production for profit, have actively countered the charismatic qualities that once provided art with its resonance and its authority. Today, power operates impersonally. We need only consult the current literature on contemporary art—catalogs filled with long lists, like computer print-outs, of every exhibition

and every collection that includes any work by the artist—
to see how our psychology of validation functions entirely
through external credentials and assertions of manic productivity. The inner biography occupies a marginal place—
even though it is the one that explains most things.

In a sense, what it all comes down to is that everything
depends on the quality of the individual. For we are what
we are devoted to, and what we are devoted to motivates
our conduct. I do not believe an artist gives meaning to his
audience. What he may give is an example of personal commitment to the search for value and for truth. To recognize
truth is not a matter of talent but of character. Among the
existential modes of truth-telling are the solitude of the
philosopher and the isolation of the artist: this is what the
modern artist understood in maintaining an independent
position as an outsider. For the majority of people, the criteria of truth are to be found embedded in cultural categories;
their identity is rooted in a one-sided adjustment to the
dominant power institutions because they have not seen
through them. Pursued as a career, art becomes inevitably
less concentrated as a charismatic activity, and less able to
break with prevailing cultural values or archetypes. Indeed,
the conceptual opposite of charismatic authority is the rational authority and power identified with administrative
bureaucracy. If we accept that the root of all influence lies
in one's inner being, then the meaning of an artist's work
can only be given out of his whole existence; in the words
of Erich Fromm, "no great radical idea can survive unless it
is embodied in individuals whose *lives* are the message."

Every civilization exhibits a certain image of man, and
we can see this image reflected in its art. A society organized
for convenience, glamour, and comfort does not lead to the
production of heroic figures. Our society lives in the image
of economic man whose desire is to increase his rewards and
cut his costs. And as modernism has been transformed into
a "profession"—big, official, capital-intensive, and bureaucratic—its heroic age has ended. The period of self-actualiz-
ing ascetics like Cézanne, working more or less alone, or of
embattled outsiders like Pollock, is behind us. Artists like
these have been replaced by professionals geared to the
organizational imperative, who feel a proper respect for all
the advantages that can be gained through official channels
and obedience to institutional procedures. In this regard, it

may well be that in his vacancy it is Andy Warhol who provides us with the truest image of the artist in our time. Compulsively addicted to glamour, openly aligned with the competition for money, status, and power, he fits into the culture as though he were made for it, allowing us to see how much avant-garde rebellion is already out-of-date.

It would almost seem, at this point, that if we could just find the right concept of the charismatic, we could somehow preserve the meaning of art. And this, in turn, might open the way for knowing what promise art holds for those artists who stand at the threshold of postmodern times. In the era of pluralism, when there are no longer any limits to what we can imagine or produce, very few people, as far as I know, have any real sense of what our art is for.

CHAPTER SIX: SECULARISM
The Disenchantment of Art
(Julian Schnabel Paints a
Portrait of God)

During 1982 Julian Schnabel was the most talked-about artist in New York. In that one year he had eight solo exhibitions and was included in twenty-two group shows, and there were no less than four pages of bibliographic references for his work. It became impossible in certain circles to attend a dinner party where Schnabel was not the center of conversation. Everybody, it seemed, was asking everybody, in an effort to get at the heart of the matter, "What do you think about Julian Schnabel?" Meanwhile, like some storybook prince with sunset-colored hair, the artist himself stood poised on the edge of his own spectacular success. Paintings which in 1977 had sold for $3,000 were now alleged to be worth upwards of $60,000. To the Brooklyn-born Schnabel, who had arrived in New York in 1973 fresh from the University of Houston, it must have seemed as if his ambition to become "the greatest artist in the world" might be realized before the age of thirty.

When a mini-retrospective of his work was mounted at the Tate Gallery in London in the summer of '82, the English art world grew similarly agitated. There was a curious sense on opening night as if the Queen of Sheba or some other great figure out of history had put in an appearance. The truth is that a certain narcissistic drama has surrounded the whole enterprise of Schnabel's meteoric career, to a point which has made even his admirers uneasy, and which seems to transcend all responses to his work. If, as many people believe, Schnabel is truly a tuning fork for our postmodern times, why does even the mention of his name set off so many unsympathetic vibrations?

"Schnabel," Robert Hughes has written in *Time,* "is immensely fashionable with collectors for reasons the work does not make clear." Surely a cultural world that for years now has been accustomed to old tires and stuffed goats as part of the normal vocabulary of painting cannot look with anything but aplomb upon the presence of broken plates and a few antlers hanging on the wall. Surely it is not the clutter of broken crockery that sets his disapprovers so much on edge, for when you get down to it, these are not threatening pictures—not in the way that Lichtenstein's comic strips were threatening when they first appeared, or Frank Stella's all-black stripe paintings. These are not radical pictures: if anything, they seem to have an old-fashioned visionary core, the subject matter ranging at times from St. Francis in Ecstasy to images of Christ on the Cross. Schnabel has even painted a portrait of God. Is it the inexplicable intrusion of religious subject matter that suggests, to those who are made uneasy by Schnabel's work, a shadowy, counterfeit practice? Or is it the artist himself that they are unwilling to endorse?

It would seem to be provocative, after several decades of self-referring abstract art, that a number of artists are reintroducing mythological and religious themes in their pictures. We can point also to the work of Sandro Chia, Francesco Clemente, and Mimmo Paladino. Are we to view this new trend as evidence of the artist's dissatisfaction with a closed secular world—as an authentic reaching out on their part for the sources of lost myths? Is Neo-expressionism a true renaissance of sacramental vision, an attempt to reconstitute a world of archetypal symbols forgotten by our society and to bring back to light their meanings? Or is it just another demythologizing tactic of postmodernism, one more form of eclectic pastiche, that merely recycles old, metaphysically picturesque images into yet another new salable genre? How can a critic, or anyone else for that matter, determine this? At this point, not unexpectedly, opinions are very mixed. Inveterate Conceptualists like Joseph Kosuth claim that Neo-expressionism, and the whole revival of painting in general, is market-oriented and regressive; while others—the critic Donald Kuspit being perhaps the most incisive among them—believe that Neo-expressionism (particularly its German axis) reinstates the power of imagination after the dry, hard-edged cerebralism of Conceptual art and the bankruptcy of late-modernist abstraction. What the new painting obliges us to decide is whether, in transferring their energies to vaguely religious characters and symbols, these artists are acting on whim, or out of stylistic necessity, or from a belief that art can have real mystical value again.

When, in the Renaissance, Michelangelo depicted God touching the hand of Adam, it was felt by everyone who saw it as a sacramental action; nor is it necessary to identify with any specific religion to experience the way this image "causes" grace, almost as if it were itself imbued with the hidden presence of God. The image hits one just where it counts. By contrast, the florid blue blob that constitutes Schnabel's portrait of God is like light transmitted through an opaque stone. Seen through the eyes of a spirituality that belongs to another state of culture than ours, it appears to have no depth to its spiritual consciousness—there seems more self-indulgence in it than visionary affirmation. If Neo-expressionism indicates a genuine struggle to liberate the visionary powers—to reclaim for art those irrational components previously suppressed not only by Conceptual and Minimalist modes, but also by centuries of modernist secularism—does it also aim to correct the spiritual imbalance in our culture? After all, if one believes in the world view of modern secularity, then it is naïve to accept the existence of a transcendent reality. And if there is no transcendent reality, then we are free to play with its symbols at will, irrespective of our prior convictions concerning the real and the divine. Symbols can be lifted out of their time and place, and plundered, as it were, for their picturesque qualities. But in the absence of any correspondence, or loyalty, to a transcendent reality, can such imagery have any symbolic value? In a society where faith has no currency, can myth be anything but banal and dysfunctional?

Schnabel, it would seem, has no particular feelings about God one way or the other—it is just another image to manipulate. Referring to one of his recent exhibitions, he explains, ". . . the paintings were all part of one state of consciousness. It had a chapel-like feeling. I wanted to have a feeling of God in it. Now I don't know if there's a God up there or anywhere. . . . Maybe I make paintings larger than I am so that I can step into them and they can massage me into a state of unspeakableness." As far as I can see, it would be a mistake to look for any visionary function on the part of these works, which seem to aim more at the artist's own emotion than at any communion with the divine. Schnabel's negative encounter with a world that has lost its divine presence seems to take it for granted that we have no proper standards for judging the spirituality of our times. What it tells us, instead, is just how much we have lost the very idea of God—how numb we have become to the experience of the sacred—and how the capacity to express religious truth seems outside the contemporary artist's horizon. Certainly, sacred symbols are doomed to make-believe and artifice in a society where their inner purpose has been suppressed and their forms deprived of any root meaning. And yet, the paradox of Schnabel's art, and part of its hold on us, is the way it frequently does seem to aspire to a numinous dimension—which poses the question of the motives from which this art has been made. If no religious impulse informs Schnabel's art, what reasons can there be today for painting St. Francis, Christ, and God?

I wrote to Julian Schnabel to ask him this, but there was no reply. The reason may be found—perhaps—in a comment by the critic Carter Ratcliff, who wrote in *Art in America* about the mythological overtones of Sandro Chia's imagery, that "the conventions of iconography are bearable in our era so long as the artist retains his privilege of confounding them. This leaves each member of the audience alone with his responsibility to speculate, to see what he can see." One of the tyrannies of the secular world view, and the penetration of rationalism into all spheres of life, is that it has become virtually impossible to raise serious questions about the existence of God, or any transcendent realm. We have learned not only to disapprove, but also to ridicule, the significance of the sacred, and to trivialize spiritual themes in which we "can no longer" believe. This loss of symbolic resonance is the peculiar degeneration of consciousness from which we suffer as a culture, and it both defines and limits the conditions of our existence. "One can be quite sure," writes Elizabeth Baker, the editor of *Art in America,* "that the iconographical nuances of much recent Neo-expressionist painting are often no more specific in their meaning to the artist than the viewer. Nor need these artists be indicted for such an attitude." Another critic, writing in *Flash Art* about Mimmo Paladino's work, claims in a similar vein that although Paladino's paintings are filled with mythological symbols, any attempt to analyze them fails, since the signs are disconnected from any source and therefore only represent themselves. And as for the supposed religious overtones of the new art, one of its main supporters and promoters, the critic and curator Diego Cortez, commented recently in *Arts:* ". . . I hate religious art. I wish it would disappear once and for all."

If Neo-expressionist works are indeed immune to interpretation, being filled with a symbolic content that proposes not to signify, it is difficult to see how they pose a challenge to, or reverse the trend of, formalism, as has been claimed. Rather, they seem to extend the formalist mode, by creating yet another aesthetic style whose primary meaning seems to be that of shifting around parameters in the art world. Beyond this context, the ultimate ground of their truth remains unclear. Not embedded in enduring beliefs or practices, locked out from any ultimate meaning, symbols can only float, gargantuan and occluded, through the spiritual vacuum created by our culture, emancipated from all conviction. It's not just a matter of recognizing that symbolic images are important, but of finding the means to animate them. Schnabel claims his paintings allude to some kind of power—the power of primitive, magical things—but you can't attach some broken plates and a pair of antlers to a canvas, pass it on to Mary Boone to sell, and hope for mythic significance. The essential inner attitude is missing —the devotional frame of mind. In addressing this issue, of the way signs of ultimate meaning have been devalued by our culture to objects of transitory and commercial interest, it seems to me that we are really addressing a much larger theme: the failure, in our secularized age, of the moral and religious impulse, and a serious disturbance in man's relationship to God.

For nearly all of human history, the world was enchanted. As material and rationalist values have gained in preeminence, however, spiritual values have declined in direct proportion. Once uprooted from the world of symbols, art lost its links with myth and sacramental vision. The kind of sacramental vision to which I am referring is not that of routine church-going or religious dogma as such, but a mode of perception which converges on the power of the divine. It is what Theodore Roszak has called "The Old Gnosis," a visionary style of knowledge as distinct from a theological or a factual one, that is able to "see" the divine in the human, the infinite in the finite, the spiritual in the material. This sacramental vision, which underlies our perception of the Absolute, can never be completely uprooted, according to Mircea Eliade; it can only be debased. However much we ignore, camouflage, or degrade art's "sacred elements," they still survive in the unconscious. Indeed, the recalling and setting up of sacred signs is the even more urgent task of an artist in times estranged from symbol and sacrament. Obviously, where the psyche is our principal working tool, the psychic attitude is of paramount importance. Before art can be successfully remythologized, we must, as a society, suspend our unbelief. And this means breaking through the terrible limitations of modern secularism.

Traditionally, artists have used art as a material means of reaching spiritual ends. Many sociologists have pointed to the fact that there is no known human society without some conception of a supernatural order, or of mystical forces governing ordinary events. Only modern Western society has taken it upon itself to discredit the mystical, believing that such "baggage" ought to be dispensed with, and that rational man should "face reality" without any superstition; but this attitude is in no way true of the original human condition. Max Weber, Émile Durkheim, and Alexis de Tocqueville all maintained that the religious impulse, far from being mere superstructure or illusion (as Marx and Freud claimed), is functionally necessary to society, and is, moreover, an indispensable mechanism of integration. "Men cannot abandon their religious faith," de Tocqueville wrote, "without a kind of aberration of intellect and a sort of violation of their true nature. . . . Unbelief is an accident, and faith is the only permanent state of mankind."

Among those who see transcendence as a necessary constituent of human life (and secularism as a dehumanizing aberration) are the contemporary sociologists Robert Nisbet and Peter Berger, for whom the decline of the sacred in human affairs is the most traumatic change man has experienced since the beginnings of settled culture in the Neolithic Age. Freud may have rejected religion as a neurotic illusion, judging the world of myth and magic negatively as errors to be refuted and supplanted by science, but as illusions they have been positive and life-supporting, providing civilizations with their cohesion, vitality, and creative powers; and where they have been dispelled, there has been a loss of equilibrium, a sense of uncertainty and nothing to hold on to. In refusing to acknowledge the reality of any experience that is not scientifically provable, the scientific world view has condemned much that is vital to culture and creative growth. To see things in this alienating way may be the particular compulsion of the modern Western mentality, but it does not necessarily reflect the way things are. Although we may value technological power more than sacred wisdom, scientific rationalism has so far failed to prove itself as a successful integrating mythology for industrial society; it offers no inner archetypal mediators of divine power, no cosmic connectedness, no sense of belonging to a larger pattern. Science, in the twentieth century, has had little to say about spiritual values; nor, it would seem, has art.

In primitive spiritual cosmology, power comes from the mysterious forces of the cosmos. Art was a form of mediation, a means of establishing contact with this spirit world and participating in its creative energies. Seen from the standpoint of the individual, the sacred has always been something emphatically other than himself, its power transmitted from a pool of ancestors and spirits to which the individual gives his allegiance, and which in turn gives his life the only abiding significance it can have. Man found his own truth by recognizing that he cannot, with any meaning, live out of himself alone. Our own secular ideology has led us to eclipse this sacred dimension—the sense of participation in a timeless reality—and to pursue immortality through the individual's own acts and works. Hubris means forgetting where the real source of power lies, and imagining, as we now do, that it is in oneself. The celebrity trades on his gifts, he does not sacrifice to them or give them away.

In modernist culture, nothing is sacred. We live in a world that is constantly more managerialized and power-hungry, but with considerable confusion as to where the power really lies. This reached fairly ludicrous proportions recently in the chicken-and-egg situation which developed over the difficulty of determining exactly who is responsible for Julian Schnabel's huge success. Some magazines have presented him as the "protégé" of his dealer, Mary Boone, who, as it happens, received more publicity in recent months than any of her artists, having been written up during the last year in *New York* magazine, *Life, Esquire, Saturday Review, Savvy,* and *People.* Being described as Mary Boone's protégé, however, enrages Schnabel, who was quoted in *Art News* as stating that "Basically she is known because of me. I think Mary is famous because Leo [Castelli] is famous. But what artist is really famous," he adds, "compared with Burt Reynolds?" "I cannot make an artist if he does not have the proper qualities," Leo Castelli comments in *New York* magazine. "But I can do it better. Mary and I. We can make an artist charismatic."

Charismatic power cannot come to anyone except from his innermost being, through the resonance of his belief in his task. At this point in our managerial society, it has become virtually impossible to balance out the simple expression of the individual against its full-scale commercial manipulation and exploitation. Belonging to a prestigious gallery that competes for the artist on the market means that all esteem earned in this way is doomed to remain equivocal. There will always be uneasiness over the significance of any success where the claims of merit are derived from power blocs seeking to secure their own dominant interest. The paradoxical nature of contemporary moral experience has been well demonstrated by Alasdair MacIntyre in his study of moral theory, *After Virtue.* MacIntyre argues that each of us is taught to see ourself as an autonomous moral agent, but each of us also becomes engaged in modes of practice which involve manipulative relationships with others. Seeking to protect the autonomy that we have learned to prize, we aspire *not* to be manipulated by others; but in the world of practice we find no way open to us to embody our own principles except through those very modes of manipulation which each of us aspires to resist in our own case.

A market atmosphere, with its constant demands for something new, is highly unfavorable to the creation of authentic and permanent values. The form of a producer-consumer society has made the world into an enclosed world: nothing exists outside it. Its ends are to be found within itself. It produces in order to consume what it produces. When this tendency becomes monopolistic, it drives out all others, and a peculiar false life, which seems the most "natural" thing in the world to us, begins to grow at the expense of more valid life. The situation is so extreme at this point that, in MacIntyre's view, belief in managerial expertise has all but replaced belief in God in our culture, and we no longer seem to have any justifications for authority which are not bureaucratic and managerial in form. Modern mass culture has tried very hard to avoid the moral and spiritual aspects of human living, and affluence has become the major alternative to religious renewal.

Our own era seems to be producing increasing numbers of artists who are content to receive their stamp exclusively from the power apparatus of the New York art world, and who, in their mode of life, reproduce the ideology of the society that molded them. Adapted to and perfectly at home in the system, they understand the language of these conditions and how to handle them; the world does not impose on them any mission beyond the realization of their own professional aims. In the life of a professional, there are no ultimate concerns, only present ones. The world is perceived as an arena for the achievement of one's own success and satisfaction; there is no struggle to realize spiritual or ethical values. And to the extent that art itself has lapsed into this function—of primarily serving the career interests of artists and their dealers—it has come to lack what used to be its unquestionable moral substance, its link with intrinsic value. To the extent that an artist seeks only personal objectives, personal satisfaction, and self-aggrandizement, we cannot say that he fulfills any moral obligation.

According to the sociologist Émile Durkheim, there are no genuinely moral ends except collective ones; behavior, whatever it may be, directed exclusively toward the personal ends of the individual does not have moral value. Moral goals involve something other than individuals: their object is society. Morality is threatened, therefore, when individualism comes to play an excessive part in the life of a society, subordinating everything else. Individualism destroys that complex equilibrium within a society whose various elements limit one another—since from the standpoint of liberal, individualist modernity, society is simply an arena in which individuals are free to pursue what is useful or agreeable to them. Certainly, much time has been spent during recent decades in denying that art has anything to do with either spiritual or ethical values. Its purely aesthetic purpose was reemphasized recently by Clement Greenberg at a conference on culture at the University of British Columbia. "It is barbarism, as Thomas Mann once said, to take aesthetic values and introduce them into questions of morality. . . . I have never felt that morality should in any sense be affected by the aesthetic factor. . . . I don't see art as having ever, in a real sense, affected the course of human affairs," he stated.

Many of our artists, suffering the repercussions of this desacralized mentality, have pretended for some time now that painting is merely a way of solving formal problems. The total opposition between art and life that formalism proposes exempts art from its moral tasks. "What is of importance in painting is paint," Jules Olitski declares; and in the same way, Kenneth Noland states, "It's all color and surface, that's all." Conspicuously missing in this "demystified" art is the mediation between God and man that has been present in art for most of its history until now. This is one of the things that makes recent modern art a thing for which there is, on the whole, no historical analogy: this act of the will which consists in man's shutting himself off against any "higher reality," or divine life. The very conception has largely been lost to artists in the late twentieth century.

In a sense, Schnabel's desire (along with other Neo-expressionists) to reinstate subject matter of a mythic and symbolic kind, and even to draw on traditional religious iconography, ought to be a corrective breath of fresh air, after so much reductive abstraction. And in many ways, it is: the mystical world view that emerges from many of these pictures strikes a lot of people as right. On the other hand, it is difficult to believe in the prophetic consciousness of someone so frankly out to get what he wants—personal success in the New York art world, not metaphysical truths. Culture-bound artists are likely to be content with the situation as they have found it, not objecting too much to the competitive demands of a system which they view pragmatically as promoting their own best interests. An artist in today's world who believes that everything is in order as long as the power apparatus continues to serve him well—who trusts the world as it now is—does not need to be equipped with moral courage. Merging himself successfully with the coming and going of the contemporary scene, having no will but that of realizing himself in his career, he can abstain from any criticism of it, because he is indifferent to what sort of future he is helping to bring about.

It is at this point that I should like, baldly, to pose a question. Can we study art for moral results as we already study it for social and aesthetic ones? I am convinced not only that we can, but that we must—that the social, the aesthetic, and the moral are inextricably intertwined, and that we have absolved ourselves of these vital connections at our own peril. Art is not value-free, as science tries so hard to be—it is motivated and purposive. When the question is one of moral worth, however, it is not the finished product which we see that concerns us, but the inner values directing it, which we do not see. We infer these values—since we cannot know them directly—from their expression in behavior. Moral philosophy offers a partial analysis of the relationship of an individual to his motives and intentions, and the intended (or unintended) consequences of his actions. The Machiavellian, for instance, does things to attain ends he never mentions or actually denies, while professing other ends which he wants everyone to believe.

The word "end," of course, can mean either an aim being openly pursued or an end incidentally achieved. Is making money, and becoming a success, a primary or an incidental function of making art? This distinction may seem irrelevant, only because our unwillingness to consider the gap between our consciously intended goals and the mode of life now necessary to achieve them has brought about a situation in which art is ceasing to serve the values it once did, and is beginning to serve other values not originally connected with its ends. For this state of affairs we tend to blame conditions, not individuals. The Kafkaesque quality of the bureaucratically structured existence is that things are done but no one is answerable for them. Unless we come to see this fact in some detail and clarity, we shall be unable to appreciate the true crisis of art in our time, or to reverse our present tendencies. Every artist today finds himself increasingly enveloped by a cultural system that makes up his destiny and requires that he act in certain ways, predetermining in crucial ways his relationship to things. More and more he finds, following the spirit of the times, that he needs to "go along to get along." Decisions become a professional rather than a moral affair. It is not difficult to see that the same situation comes into view quite differently, depending on which of these perspectives—professionalism or ethics—is applied to it. Professionalism offers a shortcut—an easy way out of moral dilemmas—because it artificially insulates the process of decision-making against the influence of more than one type of factor. Manipulating strategic factors in the environment in order to promote careers and products successfully becomes what matters. Success is operational, and any means may be used for achieving it. When bureaucratic claims and demands take precedence, the authority of morality is diminished, and its purposes in varying degrees frustrated. Everyone is reduced to being a reflex in the system.

What if we believe that *however* we act at this point, the results will be the same—that individual actions are quite helpless against the entrenched bureaucratic modes of our culture? Are we then justified in doing nothing? Obviously, no single individual is responsible for a social situation he finds himself in if nothing he could have done would have prevented it. But he may be responsible for not trying. Gandhi said the act you do may be very insignificant but it's very important that you do it. The assumption that my action will be useless does not absolve me of responsibility for the actions I might have taken but didn't. An individual who feels uneasy about events surrounding him but becomes paralyzed and unable to act is more responsible for the continuation of those events than the person who struggles to improve them and fails. The first step in breaking the bureaucratic oppression under which we are living is to develop the willingness to acknowledge that we are *all* a cause in this matter. When we view our actions merely as part of the general course of events, it seems impossible to attribute the events to individuals. But each individual is a tiny wheel with a fractional share in the decision that *no one effectively decides.* This, it seems to me, is the central problem of responsibility: that we are all responsible for the events of this world in terms of our own actions, even though it is not possible to relate these events to ourselves causally in a definite and clear manner.

What I have been trying to argue is that the artist has a basic choice as to whether or not he is to be an agent of moral transformation. In those situations where conflicting interests come together, unless we find the right means to the goal, the "good" that we seek escapes us. Social ideals of what is "good" are implicit in our way of life; they set limits to the ways and means by which we conduct our lives; they condition our sense of right and wrong, and underlie our criteria of success. Social responsibility does require some sacrifice of individualism—and a sense that one is working for society rather than for oneself.

Hannah Arendt has pointed out that whenever true authority existed, it was always joined with responsibility for the course of things in the world. The solitary shaman does not exist simply for his or her own benefit. It is precisely this exalted conception of the artist's mission that gives art its authority—the conception he has of his work, and the moral ideal to which he is committed. One of the more worrying side effects of modernism's posture of estrangement has been the generalized refusal on the part of artists to assume responsibility for the course of things in the world. As a society of "professionals," we have no objects of dedication except a specialized pursuit. Specialization, however, is what makes us feel powerless—it makes us experience everything that is outside our specialized competence as beyond our control. Arendt speaks of the "sad opaqueness" of a private life centered on nothing but itself. Authority, she states, gave the world permanence and durability, which human beings need. Its loss is tantamount to the loss of the groundwork of the world. A consumer's society cannot possibly know how to take care of a world, because its central attitude to all objects, including art—the attitude of consumption—spells ruin to everything it touches.

So what are we to do? How do we enact this vision of returning soul to the world and keeping some parts of our social, cultural, and spiritual life out of the marketplace? Obviously, we do not all agree on moral principles and on particular obligations, even if we are all more or less resigned to the business of earning a living. Does this mean, then, that basic practical conflicts have no ethical solution?

Obviously, as F. Scott Fitzgerald used to say, the test of a first-rate intelligence is the ability to hold two opposed ideas in the mind at the same time and still retain the ability to function. The subject of art and ethics has its *longueurs,* and sometimes it strikes people that I am claiming that worldly failure is the only virtue which can possibly keep the ideals of the profession from fading at this point. And if it can't be done, Gertrude Stein once nearly said, why insist on trying to do it? Why spend time shooting at pendulums?

Because, after all is said and done, moral pursuits are unlikely to advance anyone's career today, and will only produce a conflict of values which cannot be resolved, given the general state of affairs. Since everything suggests the continuation of these trends, how can we keep ourselves from becoming gifted functionaries of the system on the one hand while still managing not to starve to death on the other? Unfortunately, these questions cannot be solved; they can only be faced. But the fact that there is not a clear set of priorities for settling them in no way frees us to abandon the problem. All that can be said is that there are two obvious dangers to be avoided.

One is the danger of defeatism—succumbing to the feeling of powerlessness that makes it seem as if we are being dragged along in the wake of a system we cannot hope to challenge. To oppose this process—of resigning oneself to the fate of being helpless—is one of the crucial functions of the artist, and of any individual at this point who wishes for the survival of the world. The second is the danger of eliminating as irrelevant all moral considerations that cannot be brought within the scope of pragmatic careerism. In today's complex world, the kinds of values that motivate us are often contradictory; they will not combine readily into an easy solution determining what we should do. But the seeming impossibility of complying with these contradictory demands has led us, in many cases, to evade them altogether. Ambiguously alluring is the possibility of setting oneself against the world, turning away from it and avoiding its reality—as many of the early modernists did. Their very remoteness from the world gave them an inward distinction. The social situation of today, however, compels immersion; retreatism and rebellion are as unsatisfactory as submission and conformity. The romantic outsider, discordant with everything, will not be adequate to the task. Resistance remains essentially negative unless it leads the self beyond a mere posture of defiance. Only a personal self able to resist the tyranny of the world, by standing in ethical personal relationship to it, will stand a chance of holding out against the imperatives of the bureaucratic environment. Through our choices, changes can begin to take place in and through us. We can begin to move our world from a position of moral ambiguity to one of clarity. To be in any sense effective, however, we must proceed in conjunction with the system, but using its institutions as channels for positive change instead of for self-seeking. Only in this way can we strive for rescue from the system, even while we are enmeshed in it. We are the stewards, not the victims, of our circumstances.

CHAPTER SEVEN
Graffiti in Well-Lighted Rooms

In a world as socially complex as ours, it is hardly surprising to find deep ambivalence within the artistic community on the subject of graffiti art, which until recently existed totally outside of the cultural art scene. Graffiti art has managed to thrive on controversy, making a name for itself on insults and praise alike. For many people, the abrasive existence of graffiti on public property in New York raises a fundamental ethical question of right or wrong. From what points of view might an act of vandalism be seen as right—or justified? What makes the person who did it worthy of praise or blame? Does graffiti writing, with its indiscriminate appropriation of surfaces all over the city, represent the destructive excesses of individualism gone haywire in our culture, or is it an authentic new form of community art?

To many people, the presence of graffiti in the environment has come to symbolize violation, social anarchy, and moral breakdown. They see it as vandalism, pure and simple—a crime signifying that we can no longer take orderly society, its laws and arrangements, for granted. "I think it's a kind of theft," states New York artist Mark Lancaster, "an assault on the right to feel that public transport is a reasonable means for getting from one place to another. I think it's frightening to a lot of people. I can't separate it from fear, from someone pulling a knife on you and robbing you in a public place. You have to have an immunity to violence if you use the subways. The presence of graffiti increases the sense of lawlessness and danger, like driving through red lights, which has become normal in New York." This view is reiterated by the English artist Michael Craig-Martin, who states, "Painting the subways is a way of intimidating people. It's part of a general sense of being intimidated in New York." And in an article on the subways in *The New York Times Magazine,* author Paul Theroux recently described graffiti as nothing more than the defacement of public property—"crazy, semi-literate messages, monkey scratches on the wall," while a well-known editor of art books claims that graffiti artists should be sent to work camps.

There are others, however, who believe graffiti art represents a genuine aesthetic, the personal expression of an oppressed and disenfranchised people. The composer John Cage says we should cherish every mark; and Norman Mailer, an early and sworn supporter, wrote in his 1974 book *The Faith of Graffiti* that the phenomenon was a tribal rebellion against an evil industrial civilization, and "the beginning of another millennium of vision." More recently Diego Cortez, who has curated a number of influential exhibitions of work by graffiti artists, stated in *Flash Art* that "graffiti should be looked at as a highly sophisticated art form which is the image of New York, and is definitely the soul of the underground scene at the moment." Meanwhile, New York's Mayor Koch announced a new $6.5 million program to discourage graffiti, complete with trained guard dogs to attack artists working illegally in the train yards. His is not an aesthetic response; it is crimson wrath, burning with the logic of retaliation and revenge.

The phenomenon of graffiti is colored everywhere not only by effusions of spray-can acrylics and magic marker, but by animated, archetypal emotion. Make no mistake: the aggressive component is unnerving. Paradoxically, it is crossing the border into criminality that gives graffiti its ethical quality and its note of authenticity. Just as skulls on sticks serve as a warning to initiates in certain cannibal tribes of New Guinea that a territory has been demarcated and taken possession of, so have graffiti artists (or "writers" as they tend to call themselves) staked out their claim on this mechanical, late-industrial Underworld.

But it is not simply the appropriation of public property

that makes graffiti disturbing. At a time when the mainstream of modernism is losing its impetus, it is disconcerting to have a fringe phenomenon—a mere street subculture—enter the art market in a big way and become "legitimized." Of course graffiti has, in one form or another, been appearing in art contexts for more than a decade—imported from Harlem, Brooklyn, and the Bronx (along with its musical and dance counterparts called "rapping" and "breaking") to the downtown clubs of Manhattan and even occasionally in alternative spaces. (One of the first large-scale exhibitions of graffiti was held at Artists Space in 1975, with a catalog essay by Peter Schjeldahl.) But it only surfaced in a big way *as art* after the "Times Square Show," organized in June 1980 by Colab (Collaborative Projects, Inc.) and Fashion Moda, a South Bronx storefront gallery started in 1978 by two artists, Stefan Eins and Joe Lewis, who conceived of it as an outlet for neighborhood artists. Fashion Moda's activities were written up in the *Village Voice,* after which Eins and Lewis were invited by the New Museum to curate an exhibition of street artists from New Orleans and New York. Meanwhile, a whole new multiracial, multiethnic generation of artists was appearing, many of them from amid the desperations of ghetto life, only to find themselves suddenly pursued by important New York dealers. Another influential exhibition, "New York/New Wave," curated by Diego Cortez and held at P.S. 1 in 1981, consolidated the trend. Fashion Moda were also responsible for organizing a boutique at Documenta in 1982 to sell graffiti T-shirts, buttons, multiples, and posters.

From these few decisive events, a complex cultural archaeology has emerged. Having begun life underground, laying claim to subway cars and public walls, the unofficial graffiti subculture seems, almost more than anything else, to mark the passing of the heroic and the exalted, and to reverse the image of an "international" modernism so concentrated on "purity" that it had all but obliterated much of what was distinctive in regional art. Many issues have been raised by graffiti's integration into the institutional framework of the art world, and its consequent absorption into the success ethic. One of these is that it is no longer possible to characterize the graffiti phenomenon by one specific practice (such as spray painting subway cars), or to an exclusive set of intentions. Thus, some graffiti writers remain dedicated to an aggressive and predatory street art, whereas others—Jean-Michel Basquiat, for instance, who for a brief time wrote sentences in subway stations under the name Samo—are now more interested in being successful artists in the art world. Keith Haring is a special case, since he effectively keeps a foothold in both worlds. He is known equally for his anonymous chalk drawings on subway billboards of crawling babies and barking dogs—depicted in a hieroglyphic style that has been described as "New Wave Aztec"—as for his numerous exhibitions in Soho and on 57th Street. Both Haring and Basquiat now live entirely off their art-world work; but there are others, such as Futura 2000 and Fab 5 Fred, who remain committed to their indigenous graffiti audiences, although they have begun to attempt more visually complex statements in the context of the fine-art marketplace.

Does all this produce a conflict of values of the sort I have been trying to delineate in many contexts throughout this book? Are we confronted with yet another instance where mass-consumption capitalist economy expands into a taboo area in order to transform private behavior into a commodity? Does becoming part of the art establishment give new meaning and purpose to these artists' lives, or has it merely spawned another money-making game for its participants, while weakening graffiti's soul-energy as "outsider" art? Are these artists being rescued from a life of ineffectuality and insecurity, or have they sauntered out onto a limb that will not ultimately support them but only breed false hopes and expectations? It is difficult at this point to judge the long-term results of suddenly catapulting individuals who are ill-prepared socially and economically into a drastically altered income level—since, as Émile Durkheim has pointed out, poverty exerts its own disciplines and limits, but affluence, by its nature, usually does not. Affluence breaks down these limits, and substitutes for them a set of expectations which rise almost constantly. Are these artists being encouraged beyond any reasonable evaluation of their talents? How, finally, are we to define the underlying meaning of an experience which, to the uninitiated, appears as sheer nasty babble—at best a hermetic Morse code of hieroglyphs, at worst a violent and menacing assault?

As I talked with a number of people connected in different ways with the graffiti movement, I became aware that their attitudes did not clinch any arguments so much as illuminate different aspects of the problem, with each person giving a glimpse of the situation from a different vantage point. The first person I met with was Keith Haring, something of an anomaly in the graffiti world because he is white and middle-class and has been to a New York art school. At that point, Haring was twenty-four years old, and had been arrested several times for defacing property, although since then the police have come to recognize him as a reputable artist. I asked Haring whether becoming famous in the art world had in any way altered the thrust of his activities, or changed his intentions and goals. Did he think that working for gallery exhibitions and for big money was in conflict with his more anonymous and illegal subway activities?

"Art is about something being seen," he replied, "whether it is absorbed by the eyes of people in the subways or of people in galleries. In the subways, one needs total abandon; since the work only exists for a fleeting moment, it can and probably will be erased. The moment when it is seen may be all that is left of it. Objects, of course, have much less chance of disappearing, they will be protected, and this changes the value that is placed on them. But permanence and impermanence are both plausible outcomes to an activity. If I believed only in ephemeral things, that would be too hard a philosophy to live by; you have to believe in concrete things too, things that don't go away. There shouldn't be anything wrong with things that don't go away. There shouldn't be anything wrong with things that stay there and accumulate meaning by becoming part of someone's life. There *shouldn't* be anything wrong with that, although the situation which surrounds it does seem to pervert it. The Rockefeller wing at the Met is a perfect example of that kind of perversion, of the ability of people with money and resources to take things away which are vital to the lives of other people. The question is how good or important is it for us to see these extraordinary things compared to what those people had to lose for us to be able to do so—it's enlightening for me to see them, but it's awful for them. There is no answer, for it's a paradox; an answer would mean it was one way or the other, and anyway, it's the way things are. . . .

"I've always thought I didn't want to be paid a lot for what I do, just enough to keep things going—but there's no way to do that. If you sell your work cheaply, you just get used by the system; somebody else buys it and sells it for more, so you have to take it from them. I don't know of a way to control prices. Money's like a drug, I see it in every walk of life so far; I've not found any way to make a dent in, or alter that. In some sense, I'm already addicted. It's really hard not to be—it's such a basic idea of the world now, always to want more, to want bigger and better. And when you don't *have* to do something else to survive, it's hard to *want* to work for somebody else at $2.50 an hour, just to maintain your integrity. If *anyone* was given an alternative to that situation, they'd take it, obviously. If I say 'Things are going great, I guess,' the response is 'I'd give anything to be in your shoes.' So that even if you can see that something is wrong, someone else would change places with you immediately. Even if your own thoughts about the situation haven't changed, you find the situation has changed you, and you can't reverse that."

When I talked with Jean-Michel Basquiat, on the other hand, a twenty-one-year-old black artist born in Brooklyn of Haitian parents, he seemed unequivocally delighted with his amazing success. Basquiat was invited in 1981 by the Soho art dealer Annina Nosei to join her gallery after she had seen his work in the "New York/New Wave" show at P.S. 1. For a year he worked out of the basement of her gallery where—in something like a hothouse atmosphere of forced growth—he produced ever more prodigious paintings teeming with a psychosymbolic iconography of skeletonized figures, skulls, bones, arrows, and Twomblyesque scrawls. According to Basquiat, people are getting credit now for graffiti as if it were something new, when, in fact, they're really only fifth or tenth string. Basquiat was never part of any graffiti group; he stayed on his own a lot. At fifteen he left home and went to Washington Square Park. "I just sat there dropping acid for eight months," he said. "Now all that seems boring—it eats your mind up. Then I went to high school for a little while, where I made those typical teen-age psychedelic pictures of people's faces with stars. I was also selling handmade postcards and hand-painted Abstract Expressionist sweatshirts to make money. I even went to *Interview* magazine and bugged Andy Warhol, you know, to find out how to get closer to it. Then I was in Diego Cortez's 'New York/New Wave' show at P.S. 1. In those days I never had enough money to cover a whole canvas. I wouldn't be surprised if I died like a boxer, really broke, but somehow I doubt it. I was joking one day and thought maybe I should go to the Art Students League—to see if it's really conducive to anything—but students' work is so sad. I had more artist friends before I began to make money; now only other artists who make money want to see me. I feel much happier now—my whole life is focused. Before, there was all this energy and nowhere to put it."

Another black graffiti artist from the upper West Side, Futura 2000, took his name from a car made by Ford. Known as "the Watteau of the spray can" (although his current paintings are more like space-age Kandinskys), he has spray-painted murals on IRT trains and on the sides of buildings in New York and London. He has also collaborated with a rock group called The Clash, and shows currently with the Fun Gallery in New York. When the nineteen-year-old graffiti curator Crash first organized a show, in September 1980, for the directors of Fashion Moda —which included Futura—neither he nor the other graffiti writers were even aware of Soho. "The idea was to make graffiti on plywood," Futura stated, "to do the subway stuff on something that wouldn't be moving: it would just sit on a wall. That was the moment of transition, trying to capture the experience to be looked at in a gallery. It was the first time graffiti writers were brought above ground. Suddenly it seemed there was an opportunity for me to become an artist—not just a graffiti writer. But Soho and 57th Street intimidate me, which is why I like the Fun Gallery. I don't want to work on demand; Fun doesn't use me as a token figure. I'd be afraid to be in a big gallery where they would be trying to make money off of me—those people don't even ride the subways! My art's not for exclusive buyers. Artists in Soho get paid to produce more and more of the same stuff. I wonder what will happen to some of those people in three years. I prefer to control the level of what's happening, so it will be slower. I wouldn't mind going to art school if I could get a scholarship, but it would probably interfere with my work. . . . For lots of us, the subways remain the only outlet: a moving vehicle. The work has to be done quickly; its finest hour may be when it's just rolling by. I see the paintings more as a documentation of what goes on in the trains, a memento. Obviously, nobody can have an actual train, although in a few years' time some museum will probably buy one."

Futura is one of the "older" graffiti artists, twenty-six years old, and he began making graffiti in 1971. For years it was his whole life; he did it every day, full time, after finishing his morning job. "You can either go in with a crew or alone," he says; "that's a personal thing. I like to go with four people at most, who I know can handle the element of danger that's always involved. I always hope I'm making things look better; you never set out to destroy anything. You never go over someone else's work you respect, especially if it's something good, unless it's half gone already from the acid baths. When the trains are standing parked in a yard or tunnel is when it's best to penetrate. You can turn on the lights, blow the horn, or work with a flashlight. . . . I guess I'll always be a spray painter, but no, I won't still be spraying trains at forty. If you get caught when you're older, the penalties are much more severe. I don't want to get sent to Riker's Island, which could happen if I was caught on a top-to-bottom full-car job at night in a tunnel. But if it was all legal, it wouldn't be the same; you need the edge, the consequences of being busted."

The spectacular success and popularity of the graffiti style generated a new type of entrepreneur, personified by Mel Neulander, the organizer (together with Joyce Towbin) of Graphiti Productions, Inc., a workshop for "house-broken" graffiti artists who have been encouraged to trade in the trains for money-making canvases and worldwide commissions. Among the artists belonging to this group are Crash, Freedom, Wasp, and Lady Pink. In May 1982 Neulander held his first official exhibition of "Graffiti Above Ground," at the Stuart Neill Gallery in Soho. When I asked Neulander how he found his artists, he replied, "On the grapevine. Five or six new ones show up every week with their portfolios to join our workshop. Now we're starting to promote and market graffiti out-of-town and overseas. Our artists are prolific, well-spoken; they don't meet the stereotype of the dropout. They're not into drugs or violence. They walk around, thousands of them, with sketchbooks, doodling and drawing. They're consumed by art, but they were frustrated, with no money to buy canvas or supplies.

There's an incredible mix of kids that transcends racial, economic, and educational barriers, and they all have a tremendous camaraderie. We formed our corporation, Graffiti Above Ground, in June 1981. I had seen a documentary on graffiti on TV and loved the work. I decided to commission the kids. An article came out asking 'Is it art, or isn't it art?' When that happens, you can always be sure that, two years later, it's art. So I thought, lemme get on to the bandwagon. For me it was a money-making proposition, but I didn't know how to merchandise art, so I got together with Joyce, who had run an art gallery and been an art teacher. It took us five months to put it all together. These are ghetto children, not flower children. They want Cadillacs. They're not into the old ethic of giving up material gains to keep artistic integrity. They can do both. Now they have a market and an identity. Their needs are being satisfied by what's happening." Neulander's artists design record jackets; they did a thirty-foot mural on rollers at the Winter Garden Theater with Twyla Tharp; they were in the centerfold of a big fashion ad in New York magazine. Painting shop signs, vans, and buildings, for many of these artists, is the only alternative to mugging or drugs, given the neighborhoods in which they grew up—the only way to get out of the ghetto, where people are so desperate they are often ready to kill for a few thousand dollars.

The "upgrading" of graffiti into a commercialized art form is not viewed as salutary by everyone, however. Tim Rollins, for instance, the director of Group Material, an artists' collective started in 1979 and dedicated to promoting radical art focused on political and social issues, is quite appalled by the situation. Group Material is interested in art that is both formally and politically radical at the same time. They want to fill the gap between artists and the American working class. Among the three dissident groups—Colab, Fashion Moda, and Group Material—all have different aesthetics, methodologies, class stances, and politics, but what is shared is a desire for constructing an alternative set of social relations which will reconnect art with neighborhood communities.

"People tag Group Material as trying to develop a socialist modernism," Rollins states, "but we have a much more radical approach to materials and processes. Mural art, for instance, doesn't advance art aesthetically; murals are like coloring books for the working class. So often the whole thing is just set up in advance, and the community people fill in the colors. Graffiti, on the other hand, is extremely important. It's radical art with a radical methodology because it's illegal. It's radical because, mostly, the artists are non-artists. Formally, it's not like anything else. It's art that falls out of a social condition, and that helps us to find out about what the art means to everybody. It's not like Schnabel and Salle, who are wildly self-conscious. The problem is, of course, that now it's turning into a style, and the artists are becoming compromised by the lure of success. At the core, all that's fishy: we all worry about art being something to entertain rich people with. And so much graffiti is terrible; there are only a few who do wild and authentic work. The vitality of graffiti is in its indigenous situation. It is difficult to accept it on white gallery walls. Then it becomes part of the commodity market. The social context is what gives it its meaning, and this is being ripped from it."

Fab 5 Fred is a black graffiti artist from Brooklyn (best known for having painted a train with Warhol-like soup cans) who shares Tim Rollins' view. Fred, whose real name is Fred Braithwaite, took his graffiti name from the Number 5 train on the IRT, and was one of the first artists to put something on a train that wasn't just a name.

"The way I look at it," he says, "there've been three waves in the graffiti movement. The first wave started way back with Taki 183. He was the first person to have a name and a number. After him, there was Flowers, Dice, Super Hog; these guys developed a social network of writing clubs. Meanwhile, I was getting my shit together in Brooklyn. We all wanted to do something cool in the streets other than just breaking heads. The Ex-(perienced) Vandals, the Vanguards, Magic, Inc., the Nod Squad, the Last Survivors —these were the Brooklyn wall-writing groups. They put the name of the group up and everybody would tag around it. I got into graffiti after checking out these guys. Then the Brooklyn writers began to merge with writers from the Bronx and Manhattan. We picked up on each other's styles; we taught each other different techniques. Many styles began to merge, and out of that came 'Wild Style.' It's Brooklyn-style structured lettering with Upper Manhattan spray techniques. Wild Style is totally illegible unless you're initiated.

"I think street subcultures are a breath of fresh air. We're becoming aware of the fine-art scene, but those people approach us more than we approach them. For instance, Mel Neulander came to Futura and me. He had all these articles. He asked did we want to make money? I knew right away he wanted to make a fast buck—cheapen the scene. I definitely wasn't making any moves in their direction. Joyce and Mel encourage the artists to paint pictures of trains; then everybody comes and tags on it. They stopped taking risks. That's what I see Graphiti Productions as doing. It's like a Peter Max. It's really bad. I hope they blow away. But a lot of guys really wouldn't have any other outlet. They're not treated like real artists, though; it's like social work.

"A lot of people who approach us think we're not really hip to their game. I'm not motivated to sit on my ass for the rest of my life and be somebody else's racehorse. What I do is motivated by other things than being an art star. I want to make paintings that people from where I come from will still see that it's rooted in graffiti. That's the real beauty of the graffiti scene; it's not self-conscious like Kiefer, Schnabel, Chia. Those dudes all have the graffiti thing in their work—Kiefer slashes white paint, Chia's scribbles look like tags to me, but it doesn't have the vandalism aesthetic. . . . Graffiti symbolizes people doing what they want to do; but there's no profane language, no political statements. It's only names. Like if Jackson Pollock were around, he'd love it. I've even seen a review where they refer to Pollock as 'graffiti-calligraphy.' Calligraffiti, I call it. Graffiti isn't doing bad things, but we sort of threaten the whole notion of fine art. They think anybody not steeped in tradition has to be folk art. But New York is the most advanced ghetto in the world—what we do reverberates like a satellite, bang, all over the world. To do things in painting that have never been done before—that's my objective. That's what gives you the real good feeling. The best is yet to come. I'm working on it now."

CHAPTER EIGHT:
Has Modernism Failed?

In a film shown in 1982 at Documenta in Kassel, Germany, the English "living sculptors" Gilbert and George take turns enumerating their own characteristics. They tell us that they are unhealthy, middle-aged, dirty-minded, depressed, cynical, empty, seedy, rotten, badly behaved, arrogant, stubborn, perverted, and successful—finishing with "we are artists."

Who could ask for anything more? In the artificial, decaying environment of urban industrialism, art is not born of moral virtue; it is not meant for the saving of souls. If my attempt to throw light on the main issues of our present situation—to show what contemporary art is and does, and how it came into being—has been realized at all, it must be fairly obvious by now that ours is not a healthy society, enjoying an optimistic, conciliatory kind of art. If the modern artist once embraced modernism with hope, pride, and a crusading spirit of disobedience, at this stage of the day he seems to cling on with desperation, feeling indefinably sad and shoddy. If Gilbert and George can be taken as any yardstick, it is from his unfitness that the contemporary artist draws his power. The mood has changed from vehemence to decadence and weary cynicism. Are these words, then, a reasonable obbligato to what has become of Western cultural history—a tradition of revolt gone sour? Do they draw a fair portrait of the collective sensibility of an age dying of industrial exhaust, and without a breath of rapture?

I would betray the seriousness of the question were I simply to declare that modernism had failed, or even that it has come to a sticky end. The fact is no answer can be given without first examining what the ideals of modernism have been, and what has been essential to its system of values. What we finally think about all this will depend on what we now regard as the true end and purpose of art.

The period through which we have just lived has been, on the whole, one in which whatever was inherited from the past was thought of as a tiresome impediment to be escaped from as soon as possible. The first Futurist manifesto, published in 1908 by Filippo Tommaso Marinetti, declared that only by becoming free of "the stinking gangrene of . . . professors, archaeologists, touring guides and antique dealers," only by burning libraries and flooding museums, could Italy save itself. The new world of speed and technology required a new language of forms derived not from the past but from the future. A second manifesto declared that only by denying its past could art correspond to the intellectual needs of our time. Tradition was reactionary. Modernism alone was revolutionary and progressive.

But between that time and the end of the First World War in 1918, disenchantment of another kind set in. By the 1920s, the postwar generation of Dadaists was already doubtful—given the mercenary nature of our society, which in the words of Richard Huelsenbeck "is at best a cartel of pelt merchants and profiteers in leather, at worst a cultural association of psychopaths"—whether it was feasible, or even morally justified, to make art at all. The catastrophic effects of the war had shattered everyone's faith in a rational and peaceful future. A civilization that had condoned such inhumanities did not deserve the conciliations of art: it had lost its credibility. And so the public was baited with meaningless, aggressively absurd objects—white-haired revolvers, Lesbian sardines, vaccinated bread, and flashes of lightning under fourteen years old. The Dadaists and Surrealists wished to infiltrate a disturbed world, in order to destroy all its existing patterns, all its accumulated truth, however compulsive and authoritative.

Once art began its relentless advance into traditionlessness, every new style served as a new beginning, a new

125

plunge ahead. Beliefs had to be continually changed, re-placed, discarded—always in favor of newer and better ones, which would only be rejected in turn. (Neither science nor art in our era has been content with what has been believed before, associating traditional beliefs with back-wardness and a lack of momentum.) The "new" became the chief emblem of positive value. "Being an artist," in the words of Joseph Kosuth, "means questioning the nature of art. If you make paintings, you are already accepting (not questioning) the nature of art." The impulse to experiment continuously is profoundly different from the goal of tradi-tion, which implies a conservative attitude and considers the past as a model, or guiding example. But what the early modernists failed to foresee, in their dedication to the new, was that such a conception of history could only be built on sand, since no belief ever had anything solid to support it. Maximizing the variable of change—stimulating it artifi-cially and making it the most important thing on the stage —destroyed stability. Pressed to its ultimate conclusion, the steady violation of expected continuities—which has been the crucial element in modernist "progress"—is radically at odds with systemic wisdom and equilibrium.

To sustain itself, a society must also have values that resist change. One of the social functions of tradition has been to foster stability, and so to hinder change. The reflex of negation, in the effort to perpetuate itself as a mode of thought, has ended up destroying not only tradition, but also the art of the previous avant-garde. At this point, the possibilities for stylistic innovation seem, paradoxically, to have reached a limit. Radical consciousness has been sty-mied, along with the authority of tradition. Art must now proceed in a world that is neither structured by authority nor held together by tradition. So many metamorphoses and revolutions of every kind, so many differing values pre-sented simultaneously, have finally done away with the entire frame of things—and destroyed the conviction that there are any limits to art at all. Having thus removed any standard against which we might any more measure our-selves, we no longer know what rules we ought to follow, much less why we ought to follow them. And so the very question of what constitutes success or failure has to be an ambivalent one: it can only be judged by being measured against some valid conception of what a work of art is, and this is a conception we no longer have.

Only with hindsight can we now see that tradition and authority may be necessary, even to make a genuine avant-garde possible—in order to provide something to revolt against. At this point, we have neither: the polarizations have flattened out, and everything simply reverses into its opposite. The artist finds himself under continuous pressure to be modern, but discovers that to be modern now is to be traditional—a law of history that Heraclitus called *enantio-dromia.* That is to say, when one principle reaches the height of its power, it collapses into its opposite. Artists are finding that the only way to make something new is to borrow from the past. All this has led, in the last few years, to a disaffection with the terms and conditions of modernism—a repudiation of the ideology of progress and originality.

Traditions are a product of the recurrent affirmations that have gone into their practice. When modernism made its massive assaults on the accomplishments of the past, it deprived subsequent generations of artists of any ground plan or guidance for the future. More stable traditions of art imposed certain standards on their practitioners—patterns which were accepted as the natural and right way to do things, and which became part of the individual's practice and second nature as an artist. These standards were trans-mitted from teacher to pupil, handed down from master to disciple. This transmission is what has sustained practices and given them their history. One of the unsettling charac-teristics of modernism, as a tradition, is that it has failed to develop the means for training artists. Nowadays, the artist has no function to transmit traditional skills, or even to impart a knowledge of art—nor is there any consensus as to what should be learned. Certainly, nothing more sharply distinguishes the modern view of art from that of the past —a state of affairs that was well described by the painter Bruce Boice in a lecture I heard recently at the School of Visual Arts in New York. The talk was entitled "What It Means to Be an Artist," and Boice was addressing a group of students. "After leaving school," he said, "students often don't work, because there's no reason to work. Nobody pays attention any more, so there seems no reason to press on. There's never a reason to do art work—it doesn't seem

Failure

127

to matter—it all looks all right, but it just doesn't matter. You get bored doing it because you're in a vacuum. There's no motivation, no rules to say what you should do, or whether it's good or not. Confidence is the thing that allows you to work eventually—you know you can do this thing and succeed at it. It gets harder all the time, but you get more used to the frustration. If there were rules it would be simple enough to know what to do. But you find yourself looking for something, and you don't know what it is. So how do you ever know when you find it?"

Needless to say, these comments underline the core weaknesses of the modernist ethos—the retreat into privatism and self-expression, which means that there is no example to follow, no authority to rely on, no discipline to be received. It is almost as if the freer the artist has become, the more impotent he feels himself to be. If we accept as accurate Erich Fromm's description, in *The Sane Society*, of which human needs are basic and essential—the need for relatedness, for transcendence (a concept which for Fromm has nothing to do with God but refers to the need to transcend one's self-centered, narcissistic, alienated position to one of being related to others, and open to the world), the need for rootedness, for a sense of identity, and for a frame of orientation and an object of devotion—then the achievements of modernism would appear to have been had at too high a cost. Its renunciations of so much that is crucial to human well-being—in the name of freedom and self-sufficiency—are what will have failed us. In the end, we could not sustain these virtues without suffering their defects. Seductive though it may have seemed to escape from the world into the self, something vital has been lost along with the forsaking of reality. "Failure" is perhaps a very highly charged word—but in ways that are only gradually coming to light, something, it would seem, has miscarried.

We have obviously reached a threshold where the achievements of modernism can only really be understood against the implicit contrast of other values. The question of whether or not modernism has failed turns, finally, on the question of whether it was appropriate in the first place to reject tradition. It is just this sense that we may have taken too much to heart the drive to innovate and emancipate—regarding them wrongly as the only goals to be pursued and claiming them as the standard for all that progress and modernity mean—which has led the philosophers Edward Shils and Alasdair MacIntyre to argue on behalf of traditions as essential to the worthwhile life. The relentless emancipation from all traditions has resulted, in the opinion of Shils, in the loss of much that is indispensable to the good order and happiness of individuals. Traditions set standards from which to draw practical guidance as to what is right and wrong; they generate stable and durable systems of relationship, which help to situate individuals in the social order and establish for them a network of social obligations and responsibilities. Modernism so embraced notions of freedom and autonomy—and of art needing to answer only to its own logic, its own laws, the pure aesthetic without a function—that we now have whole generations of artists who doubt that it was ever meant to be organically integrated with society in the first place. It was during the 1950s, among the community of artists out of which Abstract Expressionism emerged, that the totally self-possessed, self-reliant individual became the model for the typical artist's role. The gesture of putting paint on canvas became the ultimate gesture of liberation—not only from political and social norms, but from previous art history as well. History (which implies responsibility to the past and a dependence on the achievement of others) was the obstacle to be transcended. A new art was necessary, and according to Barnett Newman, "we actually began . . . from scratch, as if painting were not only dead but had never existed." Harold Rosenberg wrote at the time, about Willem de Kooning, that he "discards all social roles in order to start with himself as he is, and all definitions of art in order to start with art as it might appear through him." In a similar vein, but much more recently, the German Neo-expressionist Georg Baselitz has stated, "The artist is not responsible to anyone. His social role is asocial; his only responsibility consists in an attitude, an attitude to the work he does. . . . There is no communication with any public whatsoever. The artist can ask no questions, and he makes no statement; he offers no information, message or opinion. . . . It is the end-product which counts, in my case, the picture."

Individuality and freedom are undoubtedly the greatest achievements of modern culture. But insistence upon absolute freedom for each individual leads to a negative attitude toward society, and the sense of a culture deeply alienated

129

from its surroundings. The desire for an unconditioned world can only be realized, when all is said and done, at the cost of social alienation—in the absence of integration and union. If freedom is the absolute value, then society limits, or even frustrates, what is most essential and desirable. When art had a social role—when artists knew clearly what art was for—it never functioned entirely in terms of self-interest. Today, there is a sense that only by divorcing themselves from any social role can artists establish their own individual identity. Freedom and social obligation are experienced in our world as polar opposites which run at cross purposes to each other.

But the paradox of freedom, as I have been trying all along to show, is that it is very difficult for the individual to preserve his identity in a society where traditional institutions and values offer no support. Liberation and alienation turn out to be inextricably connected—reverse sides of the same coin. Beyond a certain point, freedom—like technological progress—is counterproductive: it defeats its own ends and becomes alienating. For artists to lose the sense of being members of a tradition which transcends both themselves and their contemporaries leads to demoralization.

In its quest for autonomy and its belief that art cannot possibly thrive any longer constrained by moral or social demands, modernism discouraged the individual from finding any good outside himself. But, as Alasdair MacIntyre argues so cogently in *After Virtue*, in a society where there is no longer a shared conception of the communal good, there can no longer be any substantial concept of what it is to contribute more or less to that good. A tradition can only maintain its character as a tradition if it exists in a medium of certain virtues which impose restraints and provide a conception of excellence. A good is something that is not uniquely mine—it is bound up with the concept of observing a limit. For practices to flourish, it is necessary that they embody the virtues. In societies in which the virtues are not valued, it is difficult for practices to flourish. Modern society views discipline as a form of constraint submitted to grudgingly, but certain aspects of the moral character can be achieved only through the exercise of virtues that exist independently of each individual, and cannot be altered according to taste. The imperative quality of the rule lies precisely in the fact that it is binding—the element of choice is taken out. It requires us to act in a certain way simply because it is good to do so. Virtues are the necessary instruments which help to keep a balance between stasis and change, conservation and innovation, morality and self-interest—and which provide us with a sense of limits. It is this balance which our culture seems fatally to have lost.

Obviously, what the good life is taken to be is always relative to the individual's historical and social context. We act according to the way we see things. MacIntyre points out that the virtues are fostered by certain types of social institutions and endangered by others—cultures differ considerably in the kinds of self they enable the individual to develop. In our society, satisfaction is to be found in the vice of acquisitiveness, and virtue concepts play almost no part at all. What were vices in the Aristotelian scheme, and in the Athenian milieu—specifically, the wish to have more than one's share—is not only perfectly normal in the modern world, it is the driving force of modern productive work. Modernity emphasizes quantity—more is always better. Between the values of tradition and those of modernity, there has been a fateful conflict—a radical alteration in what the human imagination is prepared to envisage and demand. Desires, needs, and expectations have expanded exponentially. Confronting each other are not merely two ideologies, but two very different modes of being. What is required to live well and flourish in the tradition of the virtues is very different from what is required to live well and flourish in the culture of bureaucratic individualism. Indeed, the possession of the virtues—the cultivation of truthfulness, moderation, and courage—will often, according to MacIntyre, bar us from being rich or famous or powerful.

"Thus," he states, "although we may hope that we can not only achieve the standards of excellence and the internal goods of certain practices by possessing the virtues *and* becoming rich, famous and powerful, the virtues are always a stumbling block to this comfortable ambition. We should therefore expect that, if in a particular society the achievement of worldly success were to become dominant, the concept of the virtues might suffer first attrition and then perhaps something near total effacement." Within the competitive ideals of capitalism, virtue and success are not easily brought together.

131

In itself, capitalist society cannot foster a communal spirit or generate the virtues—it can only generate affluence. By now it must be clear that one of the ways in which the adversary culture of modernism has failed was through surrendering its inner independence to the pressures of external, bureaucratic power. The growing dependence on a market-intensive, professionally manipulated art world has resulted in artists losing their power to act autonomously and live creatively. This particular change happened without being instigated. It was nondeliberate. It happened because late capitalism, with its mass-consumption ethic, weakened the capability of art for transmitting patterns of conscious ethical value. And, as we have seen, this was so because often the very same artists who opposed capitalist ideology in their art were not really resistant to it; at the level of personal intention, they had a double standard, and were in complicity. They were unwilling to put their own career interests at stake in the service of convictions they were ready to accept in their art. Whether or not this process can be reversed will depend on what we all now think of the hopes and ideals with which the modern era began—and whether we believe that art is related to a moral order, or that its function is purely an aesthetic one.

Many artists, imagining perhaps that the time has come for a resolute turning away from this forced antithesis between tradition and modernism, have begun to relinquish the modernist imperative to break with the past, and are doing some antiquarian shopping in old styles. The Italian Neo-expressionists, in particular, are working in all directions—backwards and forwards, up and down. It is almost as if there were a general consensus among younger artists that, since the market has been so successful in capitalizing on innovation as a profit-making factor, the only relevant approach to the present situation is to be found in the *absence* of innovative and radical art. At this point, however, it is hard to tell. Ambiguities abound, given the even greater financial success of Neo-expressionist works. It may also be the case that for many of these artists, capitalist society is here to stay, and they no longer find the means to condemn it, or see any point in maintaining a radical position or posture. There is also the ironical feeling that complicity itself is now passed off as subversion—and being hospitable to traditional values is the most radical act.

These situations may well mirror one another, but they are not at all clear. All that postmodernism has proven so far is that something can be more than one thing at the same time, and can even be its own opposite. Obviously, the key question of the moment is whether Neo-expressionist painting is yet another symptom of our society's compulsive need to disenchant, or whether it holds the potential—however amorphous still—to restore a failing mode of consciousness. All that can be said so far is that it brings the problem to the surface in a very compelling way. Writing in *Art in America*, the critic Craig Owens, for instance, interprets Sandro Chia's depiction of the Sisyphus myth as a testimony to the painter's ambivalence about his own activity. Chia portrays Sisyphus as a comic, slightly ridiculous figure—a grinning bureaucrat in a business suit and fedora, condemned to the eternal repetition of pushing a giant boulder up the side of a mountain. In Owens' view, the myth of Sisyphus has been trivialized by Chia into a joke, and its tragic despair parodied. What we are witnessing, Owens feels, is the wholesale liquidation of the modernist legacy, in the form of contempt. Raiding the antique and commandeering the forms of tradition become the fate of the artist who finds that his avant-garde mission has failed.

If Neo-expressionism is indeed our peculiar, crippled effort to understand the lifeless symbols we inherit, the issue at stake will be how to determine which artists are merely scavenging the past and which are seeking, more actively, to influence and transform the spiritual vacuum at the center of our society. Ours is a culture in which, as the sociologist Theodore Roszak has pointed out, the capacity for transcendence has become so feeble that when confronted with the great historical projections of sacramental experience, we can only wonder what these exotic symbols really meant. After more than a century of alienation and a negative attitude toward society, art is showing signs of wanting to be a therapeutic force again. There is no doubt that a new process has started asserting itself; but the problem remains of sifting out that which is largely sensationalism geared to the media-machine from that which carries a genuine potential for developing a more *luminous* culture.

If the eclectic image-plundering of the Americans Julian Schnabel and David Salle never quite coalesce into commitment or meaning—and therefore seem more like a symptom of alienation than a cure—there are others, like the German Anselm Kiefer, whose imagery is engaged and even suggests a willingness to believe again. Kiefer, it seems to me, is one of the few artists working today who opens up the vision and ideal of apocalyptic renovation and makes the effort to regain the spiritual dignity of art. It is as if he were opening up the *fenestra aeternitatis*—the window onto eternity and spiritual clairvoyance—which in our society has been closed for a long time.

Kiefer lives in the countryside somewhere between Frankfurt and Stuttgart, and avoids art centers. Nature, in his pictures, is projected as the center of a timeless, archetypal reality—rich with symbols, evocations, and incantations. The burned and parched wheatfields, often encrusted with real hay and straw, are metaphors for a devastated earth, but at the same time—since Kiefer is almost Wordsworthian in his nature mysticism—they hold out hope for a regeneration of the Wasteland. Like his mentor Joseph Beuys (whom he once visited every day for two months, in a rare instance of genuine discipleship), Kiefer would like to bring back the ancient healing function of art. Both Kiefer and Beuys perceive that the only way to create significantly *political* art today is by making the visionary powers central. This widening of the creative field by grounding oneself in transformational vision is the only thing that can eliminate the spiritual sterility of modern life, and possibly save the world from suicide.

In a remarkable series of works, Kiefer has converted disused Nazi architecture—former Gestapo headquarters—into painters' studios. These provocative images assimilate the burden of German culture—its agony and its defeat—by transforming shame into renewal. In Kiefer's vision, art once again can be the great redeemer, a cure for the mistakes of the past; but for this to happen, not only is a mythical language of transcendence necessary, but the virtues, too, must be reinstated. In a remarkable image called *Faith, Hope, and Love,* he presents us with an image of the tree of life in which art and the virtues are one. The three theological virtues of faith, hope, and love (which were added by the Christian religion to the four cardinal virtues of the Roman world—prudence, temperance, fortitude, justice) are written on the trunks of three trees whose roots are embedded in an artist's wooden palette. In a related work, *Resumption,* done in 1974, a winged palette—Kiefer's emblem of the artistic imagination—hovers like a spirit in the sky above a grave heaped with ashes. We have a source outside the world, this art seems to say, and it is from this source that we affect the world. Kiefer's work allows no escape into despair. It is not easy optimism either, but *affirmation*—that all has not been lost, that something, some potentiality, even from the shadow of Hitlerian evils, will emerge again.

Like Kiefer, Joseph Beuys has a declared interest in the reenergizing of art's transformational power. Both share a preoccupation with images of planting and growth, with energy fields, and scenes of death and transfiguration. Beuys has described his sense of purpose as the need to provoke people and make them understand what it is to be a human being; and teaching has always been a major aspect of his creative life. But his real interest lies in the potential of radical transformation—whether of thought patterns, materials and substances, states of consciousness, or political and social reality.

In 1943, in a now legendary event, Beuys was shot down in the Crimea and rescued by Tartar tribesmen, who saved his life by wrapping him in fat and felt to help his body regenerate warmth. As a result of this experience, Beuys found himself drawn to the healing properties of these materials, which later became the basis for many of his sculptures. Among his early works are a piano which has been completely covered with felt, and a chair whose seat is covered with a thick layer of fat. These substances were deliberately chosen by Beuys because normally they would be considered unaesthetic and economically worthless. Fat expands and soaks into its surroundings. Felt attracts and absorbs what surrounds it. "It is the transformation of substance," Beuys has written, "that is my concern in art, rather than the traditional aesthetic understanding of beautiful appearances." Once he spent a week with a coyote in a New York art gallery. While the artist himself lay on the floor wrapped in felt, the coyote played with copies of *The Wall Street Journal*.

Beuys' work has always had a multiplicity of layers. He does not place primary value on the artist as the producer of his work, but on the quality of his vision and imagination —on his ability to function as a *pontifex*, or bridge-builder, between the material and spiritual worlds, and between art and society. The emphasis is always on moving art out of the private studio into a more worldly concern, in which politics and art become linked through the idea of social sculpture. Education should have the socially engaged personality as its goal, not the disaffected, dropout genius. Trying to make meaningful art in a society that doesn't believe in anything requires breaking down the rigidity of specialization, the segregation of functions and activities, both within the personality and within the community as a whole. It means reintroducing the artist in his role as shaman—a mystical, priestly, and political figure in prehistoric cultures, who, after coming close to death through accident or severe illness, becomes a visionary and a healer. The shaman's function is to balance and center society, integrating many planes of life-experience, and defining the culture's relationship to the cosmos. When these various domains (the human and the divine) fall out of balance, it is the shaman's responsibility to restore the lost harmony and reestablish equilibrium. Only an individual who successfully masters his actions in both realms is a master shaman. The artist as shaman becomes a conductor of forces which go far beyond those of his own person, and is able to bring art back in touch with its sacred sources; through his own personal self-transformation, he develops not only new forms of art, but new forms of living. By offering himself as a prototype for a new creative mode—that of a self without estrangement, able to transcend the world without negating it—Beuys shows us how we might actually achieve the possibility of a society that would maximize personal autonomy *and* social relatedness at the same time. Learning to shuttle from one wave length to another as healer, diviner, leader, and artist offers an alternative to entrapment in the web of bureaucratic imperatives and stylistic gamesmanship. Beuys seeks an enlarged vision that carries the artist outward, toward a new externality, and away from the mutually destructive relation of alienation— that reduction of the link between art and society to a purely negative function. In this sense, he provides us with a model which has passed through the fundamental errors of modernism, and whose *raison d'être* is grounded in a deeper source. In dialectical terms, the tension between traditional and modern values is resolved by the creation of an interesting synthesis of elements from both.

Obviously, it is not possible to simply give up our individuality and return to earlier times when the freedom of human action was more limited and social roles were strictly prescribed. Our present problems cannot be resolved by seeking to restrain individualism through the reimposition of traditional forms of authority, or by a regression to a past state in which they had not yet been brought into being. At this point, our possibilities rest with the use we make of our freedom—whether we decide, finally, to use it for self-aggrandizement or for moral rearmament. If anything is to change, we will need to subordinate the overdevelopment of this valued function to the dynamic good of the whole, and a new object of devotion must take the place of the present one. "I've been rich," Sophie Tucker once said, "and I've been poor, and believe me, rich is best." As long as money remains the one unambiguous criterion of success, the standards of the moneyed life will continue to prevail. The effort to get rich, and then become richer, will remain the sovereign value, as other values become weaker and weaker. The revolution in aspirations and expectations, as many have pointed out before me, must be the single great revolution of our time. It is only as individuals that we can find the way back to communal purposes and social obligation—and reconstitute the moral will. If we accept as relevant and necessary the project of spiritual regeneration, we will look for means by which we can approach art again as total human beings—not only with an aesthetic nature, but also with a moral nature, and with a philosophical and social purpose in mind.

Our art seems, in the last few years, to be leaving its experimental period behind. There has been so much varied activity over the past half-century that most prejudices have now been destroyed. The old and the new intermingle; and it has become clear that imitation and invention are not, of themselves, either good or bad. In our present state of freedom, there is no recognized means of prescribing or forbidding anything to anyone. We can see now, however, that rebellion and freedom are not enough: modernism has moved us too far in the direction of radical subjectivity and a destructive relativism. At this point we might do well to make the most of a few well-observed rules again, for this is the mainspring of all art. Only when traditional rules exist, and one is used to expecting them, can one then enjoy breaking them. Tradition teaches wisdom, and the final lesson of modernism may be no more than this: that we need a fruitful tension between freedom and restraint. The concept of the good is necessarily bound up with the concept of observing a limit. Perhaps after a long phase of rebelliously throwing out everything, we are more able to recognize that what is most acutely missing now is a sense of limits. Since immunity from the responsibility of tradition has itself become a tradition, perhaps we can go forward from the point we have reached by also going back, with a new knowledge of how form, structure, and authority sustain the spirit and enable us to live our lives with more vision; they are a necessary condition of our well-being.

It may well be that only a cultural critic who looks at the dynamics of the total situation can contain and express its contradictions—rather than taking a stand on one side or the other, or submitting to serve the ends of any particular ideological group or stylistic tendency. The role of criticism today, as I see it, is to engage in a fundamental reconstruction of the basic premises of our whole culture; it can be nothing less than challenging the oppressive assumptions of our secular, technocratic Western mentality. It is not just a matter of seeing things differently, but of seeing different things. Our culture expects us to be manic—to overproduce, to overconsume, and to waste—but in all this, something vital is missing: the knowledge that life can be transformed by a sacramental experience. For this reason, the essays assembled here invite the reader to step outside our current outlook, and its fixed investments in the soulless power-politics of cultural bureaucracy, in order to see it in perspective—to compare our world view with others, and to acquire insights that defy cultural conditioning. Direct knowing is the only thing that can break the cultural trance: deliberately and soberly changing one's mind about the nature of truth and reality, and about what is really important.

Like all ideas, the idea of modernism has had a lifespan. Its legacy requires that we look at art once again in terms of purpose rather than style—if ever we are to succeed in transforming personal vision into social responsibility again. Perhaps the real answer to the question of whether or not modernism has failed can only be given, in the end, by changing the basic dimensions in which we measure not only happiness and unhappiness in our society, but also success and failure.

CHAPTER NINE:
GLOBALIZATION
Art and the Big Picture

Conflicting opinions on the global economy are enough to keep anybody awake at night. Is it progress or rape? Where some discern an electronic global village, others can see only nightmarish global pillage. How is anyone to make sense of so many contradictory interpretations?

What the globalization phenomenon really ratifies is a shift in power from the nation state and its bureaucrats to multinational corporations and their entrepreneurs. The critics of globalization labor to point out that this transnational global flow of wealth and resources is considerably less sanguine than might first appear, since the flow moves primarily in one direction—away from the poorer countries and into the high-consumption zones of the West. It works—if it works—only at the expense of underdeveloped nations and through ruthless plundering of the environment. Globally, poverty and environmental destruction deepen inexorably as corporate profits rise. The financier George Soros has described globalized markets as "a wrecking ball, knocking over one country after another." And Indian economist Vandana Shiva puts her summary view like this: "Corporate globalization is centered on corporate profits. It globalizes greed and consumerism."

For its champions and believers, however, the globalization phenomenon represents the victory of a universal consumer society. People in the most remote parts of Borneo or the Himalayas, and in the tundras of Siberia, can now enjoy the "benefits of modernization." Via Hollywood movies and advertising images introduced through satellite TV, people around the world learn to emulate the consumer lifestyle as a culturally homogenizing ideal. Instead of participating in their own civic and community life, Eskimos, for instance, can spend their evenings watching "Will & Grace" and "The West Wing." Make no mistake: globalization is not just an economic phenomenon; it has profound cultural ramifications as well. The rising tide of American popular culture is exporting its way of life everywhere.

"Does globalization mean we all have to become Americans?" a professor at Cairo University asked Thomas L. Friedman, a leading commentator on international politics for *The New York Times*, at one of his lectures. The question cuts right to the chase. Although Friedman professes a certain "rational exuberance" about free markets and venture capitalism, he recognizes that in a world knitted together by technology, markets, and telecommunications, it has become harder and harder for countries to go on resisting globalization. We are now suffering from cultural extinction as well as from species extinction—languages and entire cultural traditions are being lost at an alarming rate. "It's like losing vital DNA," Friedman claims. Ever since the events of 9/11/2001, the globalization process, corporate dominance, and the whole ideology of modernity have emerged as the nexus of a frightening world crisis.

In *Longitudes and Attitudes: Exploring the World After September 11*, Friedman describes what he was doing when the terrorists struck the World Trade Center and the Pentagon. He was in Jerusalem, having just finished interviewing Itamar Rabinovich, the president of Tel Aviv University. By the end of the day, he claims he realized that something irrevocable had taken place, and that his two daughters would not grow up in the same world that he did. "History just took a right turn into a blind alley," he wrote in his diary, "and something very dear has just been taken away."

As I watched those buildings collapse on my own television screen in Virginia, a decades-old quote by the English writer Cyril Connelly rose up like dislodged shrapnel from a distant part of my brain: "It is closing time in the gardens of the West." Stated broadly, the destruction of the World Trade Center arrived on that day as a deadly message to the world: not everyone everywhere wants to live under the image of Western modernity and its market fundamentalism. Islamic fundamentalists in the Middle East do not want freedom, individualism, pluralism, secularism, or consumer lifestyles. To them, Western modernity and its secular ways are a lethal force threatening the loss of their own culture and community.

So what do the Big Picture—and new world developments—have to do with redefining art? To me it suggests that we need to look at, and reflect upon, the ways in which institutional structures establish the shapes and forms of what we do. In this I would agree with what David C. Korten writes in *Globalizing Civil Society*: "To move toward the creation of a world of just and sustainable societies, we must move beyond many twentieth-century ideas and institutions not appropriate to our current historical reality . . . . Our future depends on making a significant and conscious course change." I believe that Korten is right when he says that we have to find the will to take the step to greater moral and spiritual maturity—it is time to move beyond an economic model that is destroying communities, cultures, and natural systems everywhere. It is time to rethink our allegiance to what Korten calls "the suicide economy."

Weaving these elements together in the light of current developments has further expanded my earlier belief that our culture needs to define and pursue an alternative course. This matter has been a frequent theme—even an obsession—in my writing. In *The Reenchantment of Art*, a book that followed *Has Modernism Failed?*, I wrote that "Transformation cannot happen from ever more manic production and consumption in the marketplace; it is more likely to come from some new sense of service to the whole—from a new intensity in personal commitment." That book's core thesis articulated the need to approach art in ways that fundamentally reconstruct the basic premises of our whole culture. It examines the work of individual artists who have made the choice, person by person, to change into a different pattern of thinking, aligned more with the essential nature of process rather than with product.

Since then, I have come to understand that major conceptual and transformational shifts cannot just be made at an individual level. Basic institutional forms must be reconstructed as well. In this and the following chapter, I want to speak, therefore, about institutional and organizational change, some of which is already taking place.

One promising and influential figure in the art world today who is actually changing assumptions is the historian and scholar from Nigeria, Okwui Enwezor. Enwezor was artistic director of Documenta 11, an international exhibition of contemporary art which opened in Kassel, Germany, on June 8, 2002. Enwezor accepts that art's sphere of reference is now global, and he has renegotiated a corresponding curatorial approach—by emptying institutional structures of their old Kantian conceptions and making a real leap out of the old canonical system. Documenta 11 was much more than an eclectic mix of international artists from around the globe, and it went way beyond the parameters of visual spectacle. Many works in the exhibition addressed ways in which global capitalism is at the root of much of the world's anguish—but it was Enwezor's own agenda that was the driving and transformative force behind the show. At the ideological level, Enwezor not only pesters "the unyielding theology" of artistic autonomy, canons, and connoisseurship—aspects of Western aesthetic tradition and its paradigms for the organization of power. He also achieves a significant epistemological break with "the supposed purity and autonomy of the art object." In the process, he manages to redefine the relationship of non-Western cultures to the rest of the world.

Many things about Enwezor's approach challenge the ways in which art is traditionally curated—perhaps the most significant of all being his view of art as an open-ended, experimental, and discursive field, rather than a self-contained museological event. The catalogue itself—a colossus, weighing in at seven pounds and containing over 600 pages—immediately gives the sense of art throwing itself out into the world and moving forward in a new dialectical relationship with the global culture at large. Enwezor's approach is shockingly strong. The first thirty pages of his catalogue consist of a disturbing spectacle of images—photographs from global news agencies that confront us with war and social chaos, poverty, disenfranchisement, and endless amounts of rubble on the ground, from New York to Ramallah—as a kind of visual vernacular for the mass unrest and fragmented politics that have become our world. (A photograph of Palestinian president

Yasser Arafat donating blood in a Gaza hospital to aid victims of the terrorist attacks in the U.S. is one particularly telling example.) This lexicon of images immediately sets us in present time, and acts as a useful starting point for putting us face-to-face with globalization and its damaging effects on the lives of the world's people. Enwezor is not shy about using art as an entry point for the biggest social, political, environmental, and ethical questions of our time. He doesn't see art and politics as separate. Documenta 11 was in every way a benchmark event, encouraging people to open their minds to an unprecedented mix of ideas and influences from a dizzying variety of sources.

In an effort to break down the institutional authority attached to the site at Kassel, Enwezor orchestrated Documenta 11 in multiple zones of activity. In order to open up dialectical interaction with transnational audiences, he created five different thematic platforms (public conferences, film and video programs, workshops and lectures) that were staged in five different cities: Vienna, New Delhi, Berlin, St. Lucia, and Lagos. The intention was to "deterritorialize" artistic space and discourse and to globalize it. Western art history, in particular, and the academic and institutionalizing procedures connected with it, are woefully inadequate to deal with the forces that today are reshaping the values and views of a global sphere—forces which now traverse continents and cities, locations and disciplines, practices and institutions. In seeking to build a "deterritorialized understanding of culture," with multidisciplinary directions that exist outside the institutional domains of Westernism, Enwezor's agenda goes far beyond the parameters of the culture wars of the '80s and '90s, which sought to include the art of other cultures as historical supplements within a single, universal narrative frame. That narrative frame understands the forms of art by separating them from the world and linking them, instead, with each other. Given his post-imperial, post-colonial outlook, Enwezor prefers to view himself as a curator of cultures rather than of canons.

Extending over a time frame of eighteen months, these multidisciplinary events, described by Enwezor as "research modules" or "interlocking constellations of discursive domains," allowed individuals from a variety of disciplines—philosophers, activists, theorists, historians, psychoanalysts, and writers—to exchange ideas and discuss critical methods and ways of thinking that might ultimately lead to a sense of global culture more like an emerging wave than a system of hierarchies. Enwezor understands that culture does not have a uniform effect on all societies that experience it. Developments in China, South Africa, India, and Nigeria frequently suggest practices, models, and experiments that, in terms of the gallery-museum system, may seem hardly recognizable as art. Platform 4, for instance, entitled "Under Siege," studied four African cities—Freetown, Johannesburg, Kinshasa, and Lagos—all of which have undergone state and economic collapse, partly due to programs instituted by the IMF and World Bank, which destroyed the local economies. Platform 5 was the exhibition itself at Kassel, a genuinely "worldcentric" compendium of over 160 artists or artists' groups.

One of Enwezor's co-curators, Sarat Maharaj, suggests in his catalogue essay that, instead of treating different cultures in a single frame, we make use of "xeno-equipment"—a term he invents for a new grammatical lingo that will elude the ready-made art categories and received classifications of "Kantian, 3D knowledge grids." Language has a dual character, as both a means of communication and as a carrier of culture. Through disturbance and commotion at the level of language, one can achieve a changed sense of art itself. Xeno-equipment seeks to break through the rigor of disciplinary boundaries and methods, replacing them with an open-ended "unscriptedness." Maharaj writes, "the sky's the limit; anything can become the receptor-conductor of art practice." Documenta 11's "para-epistemic probes to whip up see-think-feel weather fronts" were quite effective in opposing the academicizing, standardizing, and commodifying trends of our culture.

It must be said that Enwezor's contribution to artistic discourse is not without its fierce bite marks into the whole notion of Westernism—defined as all those institutions devised and maintained solely to perpetuate capitalism and the vision of secular democracy as a world system. The message is: no subservience. Resistance and liberation struggles today are often centered in societies trying to prevent themselves from being incorporated into the

Western world system, which is promulgated as the only viable form of social, political, and cultural legitimacy. "It seems quite clear," he points out in his catalogue essay, "that the West had completely underestimated the ferocity of fundamentalist Islam's hostility toward Western hegemony."

For Enwezor, Ground Zero was a defining moment, a ground-clearing gesture of tabula rasa, forcing Western culture to redefine itself away from the dichotomizing perspective of "the West and the rest." Enwezor casts his own fertile spell over this dichotomy and leapfrogs right over it. We could, he suggests, use this moment to make a radical departure from the system of hegemony that fuels the present struggle. We could even frame Ground Zero as the instance of the full emergence of the margins to the center, the moment when frontiers between geographies and cultures became permeable.

It is interesting to contrast Enwezor's response to Ground Zero with that of another art-world figure, the art critic Dave Hickey. Hickey is, of course, our most hyper-enthusiast of postmodern artistic chinoiserie. At the time of his much acclaimed exhibition, "Beau Monde" (held at SITE Santa Fe in the spring of 2002), Hickey was interviewed in Las Vegas, where he teaches, by journalist Matt O'Brien, who asked him: "Has the definition or meaning of art changed since September 11th?" To which Hickey replied:

"To be honest, I have no idea. If you want a commentary on the terrorist attacks ask an actor, ask a folk singer. They're trained in cliché, and they're the ones doing all the commentary. I'm sure it will make things very stupid for a while. But I grew up in the '60s, so I'm used to people being blown up. My students are having nightmares, but it's just the same old shit to me . . . . I'm not in the prediction business. It certainly hasn't changed the meaning of art. Art is what it is . . . . People being murdered is not really an art issue." I deliberately place these comments here because their signature posture of recoil and neutrality stands in perfectly for the old modernist idea: art cares not if it truly knows the world. It only wishes to make an interesting art object. In Hickey's case, he has always worn the posture well. But sometimes, when the timing is wrong, even flashy barroom humor can be stupid just when it needs to be smart.

If Okwui Enwezor has emerged on the scene as a prominent globalist, using the forces of globalization as a means to shake off Western hegemony, Thomas Krens, ever since he became director of the Guggenheim Museum in the late 1980s, has proved himself to be a different kind of key player in the global sphere. The difference is that whereas Enwezor's approach is a leap out of the old system, Krens has capitulated and jumped straight onto the globalization bandwagon. Responding in part to the expansionist economy of the 1990s, Guggenheim Museum franchises are being exported around the world on an unprecedented scale, with branches in Venice, Berlin, Bilbao, another already under construction in Las Vegas, and one projected for Rio. "Global Guggenheim" has become a logo, like Nike, Gap, and Disney. It definitely is not seeking a value system outside of the machinery of corporate commodity capitalism. If we are to believe Krens's logic, there is no longer any alternative to the capitalist system—we are trapped in it, so resistance is futile. Thus, instead of deploring the state of affairs, the smart move is to embrace it opportunistically. Krens has no anxieties about defining himself as a corporate globalist who believes globalization is beneficial and inevitable. He has no problem filling the world up with American monoculture. In the new global economy, museums can become tourist magnets and circuits of global power. Guggenheim Bilbao, for instance (and here I am much indebted to an excellent essay on the corporatization of museums by Michael Brenson), has drawn 1.4 million people a year since it opened in 1997, and has given a major economic fillip to the entire region. Ambitions for art have never been higher. So much so that now, Krens claims, "we have requests from every continent except Antarctica to build Guggenheim museums." Bilbao has become a site of contemporary pilgrimage—at least according to Krens, who likes to bill it as "the Chartres cathedral of the 21st century."

In his essay, Brenson points out the unconcealed corporate imperialism in this new proof of cosmopolitanism. Corporate patrons like BMW financed the 1998 "Art of the Motorcycle" exhibit, and Giorgio Armani allegedly contributed $15 million to the exhibition of his own fashion designs in 2002. Not only are these museum franchises around the world "ultramodern showcases" for brand-name corporate trend-setters, but they are all controlled from New York and serve market-oriented mainstream art and culture, not local interests or histories. What appears to be life at the cutting edge is really no more than a relic of elite privilege.

In the wake of 9/11 and recent corporate scandals, the Guggenheim has had its share of financial setbacks, employee layoffs, and canceled exhibitions. Something about Krens's symbiotic relationship with the dominant corporate culture seems to have touched a sensitive nerve of repugnance in the art world. In fact, while surfing the Internet for material on Krens, I had to wonder if he had become the Trent Lott of the art establishment—someone whose values were now an embarrassment to the party. There were several harsh indictments of his expansionist quest and alliance with the world of megacorporations flaring in cyberspace.

"It is time for Guggenheim director Thomas Krens to go," stated one e-manifesto by Jerry Saltz, an art critic for the *Village Voice*. "The trustees and board members who helped him twist this institution into a kind of GuggEnron should go as well .... Krens & Co. have turned this already fragile museum into a rogue institution, broken faith with art, and stripped it of the reputation won for it by generations of artists and curators." That text was almost a year old when I found it, but another had been put on the net that very day by the *New York Observer*: an article by Hilton Kramer entitled "Guggenheim Is Bust—Why Isn't Krens Getting the Boot?"

Kramer charges Krens with selling off the Guggenheim's "permanent" collection to support his spendthrift expansion programs here and abroad, citing sales figures reported in *The Wall Street Journal*. He assails Krens's "tomorrow-the-world ambition" to create an ever-expanding, ever-more-costly Guggenheim empire, with satellite museums in Europe, Asia, and South America, "not to mention the ill-fated attempt to set up shop at the casino in Las Vegas." Kramer laments the era of the modern masters and the authoritative catalogues that accompanied their exhibitions in the past under previous curators, and views the current disastrous state of the museum as "a casualty of Mr. Krens' overreaching ambition." Krens, of course, is still around, seemingly impervious to these assaults.

All of which brings me back to the central theme of *Has Modernism Failed?*: the mismatch between the imperatives of corporate capitalism and art. The great struggle between the world of culture and the reward systems of the world of money is far from resolved. Once the profit motive is viewed as the purpose of human existence, money becomes an all-consuming and increasingly self-destructive obsession—and nothing can change for the better. For this reason, my attention has turned increasingly toward a deeper exploration of institutional alternatives, and toward those who are defining new paths. Adopting this position, I believe, is the only way to take the conversation to a new level.

CHAPTER TEN:
TRANSDISCIPLINARITY
Integralism and the New Ethics

How do individuals overturn a world view based on competition, exploitation, and profit, and break free of its limiting ideologies? And (last but not least), where do spiritual and moral values fit in? In this final chapter, I shall look to the possibility of finally trying to answer these crucial questions.

For most of my lifetime, there has been an awkward, even a rigid, dualism between aesthetics and ethics—just as there has been a split between subject and object. In the same way that science aggressively rejects religion, modern aesthetics has rejected ethics, as if the truths of the two realms were somehow mutually exclusive and had little in common. Few people are willing to talk about ethics and aesthetics in the same breath. Aesthetic autonomy is a deeply rooted idea—autonomy implying moral and social separateness as the condition of art-making. Kantian and Cartesian epistemologies keep all the categories split up, but with a different, more unified vision of the world, art and ethics can perfectly well coexist and cooperate.

In his book *A Theory of Everything*, Ken Wilber puts forth a world philosophy that weaves together the many pluralistic contexts of science, morals, aesthetics, Eastern as well as Western philosophy, and the world's great wisdom traditions, to suggest that the world is one undivided whole, and related to itself in every way. The well-being of each part is the responsibility of every other part. Referring to the earlier cultural movements of traditionalism and modernism, Wilber suggests that *integralism* is the next big

149

developmental step. "Integral" conveys a sense of responsibility to humankind as a whole and to all living beings. The idea of integralism involves some very real changes in perception and understanding that have been occurring over the past twenty years. I would claim that a more ethical artistic vision is already functioning among us. Founded in dynamic models of integralism, intersubjectivity, and transdisciplinarity, this new artistic culture no longer depends on the primacy of the dealer-collector-critic-curator network, but replaces it with very different kinds of networks. And in the way this culture deals with the world and actively shapes reality, it also corrects any assumption that consumer capitalism is now like an inevitable force of nature, rather than the product of particular individual and social choices.

Simply by altering their aims, artists can wrest art from its familiar institutional contexts, to realize what the Roman mystic Plotinus called its "amphibious nature." Models of transdisciplinarity and integralism provide a new kind of lens through which the inherent, dynamic relationship between aesthetics and ethics becomes one contiguous practice, while the separate truths of each can mutually enrich each other. Separating art from ethics (and from life) has distinct advantages, but it also gives a damaging impression of clear boundaries and a misleading impression of two opposing camps. I have come to believe that this separation is arbitrary. What follows here is a handful of practical examples to give the notion of integralism and transdisciplinarity a discernible shape. I think they represent a serious ethical basis on which to set a new course.

In December of 2002, I received a letter from a potter named David Levy, describing his personal struggle to combine work in ceramics with his concerns about the world. "I am finding it increasingly difficult to engage in the making of pots as objects to sell," he wrote. "This is not enough. Objects once served humanity and held a more meaningful place in our lives. Is there a way of raising our voices, our values, as living objects, beings with heart vessels?"

The answer to Levy's question arrived when he learned about the Empty Bowls project, founded in 1991 by a high-school art teacher and potter, John Hartoum, and his wife, Lisa Blackburn. The couple were looking for a way to help

Hartoum's ceramics students support a local food drive for the homeless. The basic premise of Empty Bowls is simple: guests are invited to a meal of bread and soup, served in handmade ceramic bowls, in exchange for a cash donation. Food may sometimes be donated by local restaurants. The guests are invited to keep their bowl as a reminder of the meal's purpose—to eliminate hunger worldwide. Monies collected are donated to an organization fighting hunger, chosen by the people involved in that particular event. Information packets are provided beforehand with instructions on how to orchestrate the event, including follow-up forms to track its specific nature, the amount of money raised, and where it was donated.

What is especially notable about this project is the way, having started as a single, one-off event, it has since grown into a major nonprofit organization. Now called The Imagination/Render Group, it has raised literally millions of dollars to combat hunger. In 1992 an Empty Bowls meal was held in Washington, D.C., at Oxfam America, and since then, Empty Bowl events have been held across the U.S., in New Zealand, Canada, and Hong Kong. Their tenth-anniversary celebration in 2000 included a national exhibition at the Peace Center and Gallery in Detroit, which featured 250 handmade bowls, the combined work of potters, art students, and social justice advocates. In Maryland alone, the Center for Poverty Solutions (CPS) has raised $450,000 over eight years through an annual EB fundraiser. Estimates are that more than $2 million has been received nationwide to alleviate hunger.

This project honors the world by really seeing it. No aesthetic canons need to be dragged in by the hair to bestow legitimacy. Its very spareness and simplicity touch a nerve. Empty Bowls has become an advocacy teaching tool, used in schools at all levels. Its strong educational component is intended to build a sense of civic and social responsibility and to explore the politics of hunger in an affluent society.

A sentence of mine from *The Reenchantment of Art* has been cited by the directors as a pointer for the project: "We need an art that transcends the distanced formality of aesthetics and dares to respond to the cries of the world." Inspiring long-term commitment to service is an integral part of the Empty Bowls project—using art to effect positive social change. David Levy brought the project to the Academy of New Paltz, and now faculty and students participate annually in an Empty Bowls event. Levy feels it is an opportunity for young people to expand their views about life and art, putting their creative skills into serving people in need. "A simple beacon of light," he says, "to cut through barriers and divisions, and show a path to our human heart."

In his *Manifesto of Transdisciplinarity*, theoretical physicist Basarab Nicolescu argues that reality is not something that exists only on one level. Rather than the self-sufficiency of each discipline unto itself, Nicolescu advocates a transdisciplinary approach that can deal with the dynamics of several levels of reality at once. He is careful to distinguish transdisciplinarity from multidisciplinarity (a way of widening the frame of a particular discipline) and interdisciplinarity (transferring methods from one discipline to another).

The point about the transdisciplinary approach is not just that it traverses disciplines, but that it deals with the dynamics of several levels of different and even mutually exclusive realities (ceramic arts, say, and hunger; aesthetics and ethics) at once. Also, it has a unique goal: to propel us beyond either/or thinking into a coexistence of nested truths. In this model, no particular discipline is privileged, since they are all integrated into an open unity. Of course, it is likely to provoke the old catchword question, which always hangs around these discussions like a migraine: But why is this art?

No matter how much the notion of the artist is expanded and redefined, many people are still only comfortable with the image of the artist as a maker of objects circulated in a network of art-related institutions like galleries and museums. My own reaction to such a clear-cut definition is of course to reverse it. How many artists feel free to work outside their field? How many are willing to blur the distinctions between art and life—to muddy the waters of art and create a healthy confusion of genres?

I believe we are slowly moving away from what Nicolescu calls "the era of the disciplinary big bang and relentless specialization." Strategic changes are happening in which the individual artist becomes an integral component of a larger social network. Specialization may still be the most general trend we know, but a significant number of artists have extended artistic activity into social and environmental domains, transcending disciplinary boundaries. Not surprisingly, institutions have begun to follow suit.

The key metaphor here, as I will try to show, is that of the *network*, both as a new pattern of organization and as a generative creative force. One example of the kind of institutional change I am talking about is the ARTS UP program of the Seattle Arts Commission, headed by Lisa Richmond. ARTS UP pairs artists from around the country with communities of all descriptions, connected either by a geographic location, a cultural or ethnic background, or a common challenge or interest. Once paired up, the goal is to engage in civic and artistic dialogue. In 2000, the Commission issued a national call for artists with a demonstrated commitment to working collaboratively in communities. ARTS UP now maintains a roster of artists that includes sculptors, performers, writers, composers, filmmakers, and conceptual artists, who have been preselected by a panel. When a community in Seattle with a certain set of interests or challenges begins a project with ARTS UP, they select an artist from this roster to work with them, and together they develop a project proposal. Projects vary in size and scope, and will often involve a coalition of organizations and funders. They may include anything from physically improving low-income or immigrant neighborhoods by creating community gardens or murals, to exploring local histories and stories, and then preserving them through multimedia design, film, or videotapes. Currently there are fourteen ARTS UP projects in various stages of development, all of them founded on the idea that art can have a vital role in community building, and in giving voice to those whose lives are otherwise unrecognized or isolated.

Someone else who I believe has bent the museum into a new and interesting shape through the use of collaborative and networking programs is Susan Lubowsky Talbott, currently the director and CEO of the Des Moines Art Center. This museum has always been an especially beautiful place, with each of its three wings designed by a different architect: Eliel Saarinen, I. M. Pei, and Richard Meier. It houses a remarkable collection of nineteenth- and twentieth-century art. But perched high up on a hilltop several miles outside of downtown, it had a reputation for being a bit aloof, elitist, and not very welcoming to the city's multicultural community.

Can the museum be a test site for piloting economic and social alternatives? Talbott, who had already proven her participation-building skills during a previous tenure at SECCA (Southeastern Center for Contemporary Art) in Winston-Salem, made it her mission, when she came to the Art Center in 1998, "to get rid of every last vestige of elitism." Borrowing a phrase from Arthur C. Danto, she wanted to create a museum that would be the "defining social center" of her community. And it is now easy to see that she has achieved her goal. One might even go further and say that the Des Moines Art Center has become a notable and innovative example of integralism and transdisciplinarity: it combines exhibitions of art-world alpha stars like Eric Fischl, Andy Goldsworthy, and Martin Puryear with other kinds of dynamic interchanges that relate to the community in a more participatory way. The museum collaborates extensively with many local organizations and local artists. It has begun translating press releases and gallery guides for exhibitions into as many as six different languages. Community days for audiences of all ages are planned, that include refreshments, workshops, and music, as well as summer day camps and creativity days for children. A "Day of the Dead" celebration in November 2001, for instance, attracted nearly 2,000 long-neglected constituents from the Latino community, with a bilingual program that included live music, family art workshops, storytelling, and a program honoring the lives of departed local Latino leaders.

As part of the museum's ongoing artist's residency program, visiting artist Ivan Fortushniak worked with elderly persons living in a local senior citizens' residence for nine weeks, helping participants create collages that captured aspects of their personal histories. Their work was later exhibited, with receptions held at the home and at the Art Center. One of the residents reported that her artistic experience there had really opened things up. "People weren't just talking about pills or doctors or operations. They spoke about memories they hadn't talked about for years because they'd thought, 'Oh, nobody wants to hear about this.'"

My sense is that significant changes in power relations are occurring, as these decentralized network structures now offer the possibility for artists to interact with each other, and share information, in a democratic and cooperative atmosphere that was mostly absent within the hegemonic, competitive, institutional structures of modernism. The phenomenon of networks as a new pattern of organization is nowhere more evident than among the many different "communities of practice" to be found on the Internet. Virtual communities offer a collective identity for their members, who usually bring to the group a shared vision and purpose. These living networks have become so widespread that they are even breaking the stronghold of individualism in the dynamics of culture, in favor of a new communal "we."

Included in the category of "netcentric" collectives is Samuel Bower's greenmuseum, a nonprofit virtual museum of environmental art that serves as a highly interactive resource for artists and educators. Greenmuseum supports collaborations and interdisciplinary problem-solving, and encourages strong bonds of sharing among artists who love nature and want to create an honorable place for the idea of art as service. It publishes new writing, describes artists' projects, promotes on-line forum discussions about eco-art, prints out course descriptions by educators, offers links to artists' websites, and announces exhibitions.

In 2002, greenmuseum collaborated with another on-line environmental organization, ecoartspace, to produce an exhibition of environmental art called *Ecovention*, at the Contemporary Art Center in Cincinnati. In conjunction with the exhibit, they co-published a catalogue which offers an overview of artists who have been engaged for more than three decades with the reclamation and restoration of damaged ecosystems. These projects involve strategies drawn from many disciplines, and invite collaborations with specialists such as architects, botanists, zoologists, engineers, and local city planners. *Ecovention* presented these projects as case studies that pave the way for "a new kind of art that can help realize needed change in the world."

"There is a small yet growing world wide movement of artists who are actively at work finding ways to creatively solve ecological problems," Amy Lipton writes in her

155

introduction to the catalogue. Lipton is an independent curator who, in 1997, began a search "to find artworks that cross the line from traditional art production and institutionalization into the larger context of human and non-human communities." Lipton was looking for a kind of relevance she failed to find in the art circulating in galleries that sometimes addressed problems like AIDS or gender identity, but never seemed to engage with ecological issues. Ultimately Lipton co-founded Ecoartspace, another nonprofit organization (with branches on both the East and West Coasts), in order to support artists who create works that raise environmental awareness. Ecoartspace curates exhibitions, works in educational contexts to implement art-and-environment curricula, acts as a consulting resource for artists and museums seeking to address ecological issues, and seeks to create a cooperative ethos of teamwork.

Once again, I expect people may object. What link can there possibly be between concepts like "endangered species," renewable and nonrenewable resources, damaged forests—and the problems artists have to face in building successful art careers? What do art and issues of chemical contamination have in common? A case in point is the comment by Robert Morris, quoted in the catalogue: "Why should site-works be seen as relevant by a community only if they fulfill a kind of sanitation service?" Presumably the question is intended as a veiled slur on reclamation projects by artists who work with sewage treatment plants, landfills, brownfields, and slagheaps—such as Mel Chin, for instance, a sculptor who uses plants as remediation tools to absorb large concentrations of metals and minerals from contaminated landscapes that help to restore them back to health.

Morris has a point. We are not used to defining art as research, or having environmental cleanup seen as its legitimate goal. Ecovention cannot be easily absorbed within the prevailing ideology, and if truth be told, it is a world apart from land- or site-specific art, because of the ethical issues of responsibility it deliberately embraces. "If it doesn't actually change the world," Tim Collins declares in the catalogue, "it is simply not an ecovention."

Collins is an artist who focuses on restoring and preserving polluted rivers and ecosystems along the postindustrial waterfronts of the Allegheny County area of Pittsburgh; he sees his work as following in the footsteps of the restoration projects of eco-artists Newton and Helen Harrison. Collins is also a Research Fellow, one of five full-time artists contributing to collaborative, transdisciplinary enterprises under the auspices of the STUDIO for Creative Inquiry, at Carnegie Mellon University. In the context of institutional changes, this, too, is a program that bears watching.

The STUDIO for Creative Inquiry was founded in 1989 and is international in scope. It describes itself as an arts service organization, functioning as an academic home to a range of artists with backgrounds in the visual, music, architecture, design, and performance arts. Tilted strongly in the direction of social engagement, with an intention of impacting local and global communities, the STUDIO integrates the arts with engineering, technology, new media, and the natural and social sciences. Its mission is to serve society through attention to the social fabric, and, using the administrative, financial, and knowledge resources of the university, to further the processes of creative inquiry, transdisciplinary research, and artistic expression. Within this structure, art is an active and integral praxis that involves problem-solving, teamwork skills, and ethical commitment. The goal is to insure that individual creativity is engaging with the important issues of our time. Currently the STUDIO has seven projects in development, and artists directing them have secured over $4 million in grants, many from outside funding sources. Philosophical and artistic direction is provided by a steering committee, composed of department heads from the College of Fine Arts, which oversees all decisions and mediates with the university.

Another significant instance of this new network pattern—characterized by synthesis, cooperative team work, the bridging of organizations and of hybrid areas of knowledge—can also be observed in *Watershed*, a project originally launched under the auspices of Minetta Brook, a nonprofit arts organization in New York City, founded and directed by Diane Shamash. *Watershed* functions in partnership with a number of other cultural, environmental, and civic organizations, including the Dia Center for the Arts. In 2003 several major cultural institutions opened auxiliary branches in Beacon, N.Y., a former manufacturing center for the brick and textile industries, whose empty mill buildings and storefronts on Main Street are now being converted into galleries and museums. (The Dia Center, for instance, is transforming an abandoned Nabisco-box printing factory into a subsidiary museum in Beacon.)

What sets the *Watershed* project apart from other upscale urban renewal programs, however, is its transdisciplinary purpose: *Watershed* represents a new cultural engagement with nature and ecology centered around the geography of the Hudson River Valley. Already well known and admired through the "sublime wilderness" paintings of Hudson River School artists like Thomas Cole, Frederic E. Church, and Albert Bierstadt, and through the novels of Washington Irving and James Fenimore Cooper, this landscape is currently getting a new lease of life. The fundamental idea behind *Watershed* is to reinstate the scenic legacy of the Hudson River Valley in the public imagination. Ten artists have been commissioned to develop participatory projects centered around the history and communities of towns along the Hudson River. Though still in the planning stage, a few of these projects warrant at least a brief description here.

Lothar Baumgarten, famous for his site-specific works evoking the loss of indigenous history, language, and culture in the Amazon, is using the site of a 67-acre wooded peninsula close to the Dia Center to record a CD from the seasonal sounds of birds, toads, insects, ice, rain, etc.— some of which may predictably be extinguished in the course of cultural encroachment. Baumgarten's *Watershed* project will also include sculptural installations that create circular-form gathering places along the shoreline and woods, where people can sit and listen to the sounds of wildlife. Another artist, George Trakas, whose art often takes the form of bridges, pathways, and docks, will make the waterfront at Beacon Landing more accessible with a series of granite stairways to the water, a dock area, seating and fishing areas, and a community boathouse. German artist Christian Philipp Muller is building an earth sculpture of local soil samples from different counties on the grounds of Bard College, and he will produce a cookbook focused on edible plants, berries, and herbs of the

Hudson River Valley, that will also include portraits of local farmers, restaurants, and chefs. This three-year program of commissioned art works will be combined with special events (orchestrated by Lynne Cooke, Sandra Percival, and Lynne Tillman) to be staged at the region's farms and historic vineyards along the seventy-mile stretch of the river between Bear Mountain and Hudson, N.Y. In addition, special internship programs at five nearby colleges and universities such as Bard and Vassar will stimulate collaboration between artists, students, and different cultural, educational, historical, and civic organizations—all of whom will aid in the creation of art works, films, performances, special food events, and educational seminars relating to the history, geography, and industries of the Hudson River Valley.

All of this clearly represents a critical shift in the definition of an art object. These networking social processes, which integrate complex pluralities into an open unity and bridge many different areas of knowledge, also require a real rewiring of institutional DNA. The arc of specialization has been displaced by another organizing principle—decentralized creativity—in which the individual artist becomes a structural component in a society of selves that fit their contributions together in mutual enrichment. We have truly entered here into "the era of the integrative approach."

In a personal conversation with me, Tim Collins shared his view that the self-referencing discourse of modernism, with its unilateral focus on fine art, has become tedious and circular for many artists who now embrace post-studio practices. Almost in spite of themselves, artists tend to fasten on galleries and museums as the penultimate repositories of art's truth and goodness. Collins believes, as I do, that within capitalist democracy, cultural production has become a monoculture, so the issue for him has become how to add diversity to this ecosystem. As an eco-artist, Collins tends to frame his thinking in ecological and biological models. "How do we diversify our own thinking in order to get off this singular path of market-based object production—along with its self-limiting notion of freedom of expression? How do we create new institutional forms, or else, through interdisciplinary practices, breach the existing forms to discover new options?"

One obvious path out of the "autonomy" bag, and the resistance to integralism, is to understand that art needs no fence. Going outside their own discipline is one way that artists can introduce new levels of diversity. As Collins observes, by creating models of diversity and putting them in place, you can also complicate the discourse in meaningful ways. The purpose of this is not to disparage what others are doing. Rather it is meant to open up new options and lead to the understanding that art can be many things at once. The intent is to enrich, not to force these ideas on anyone. As Collins himself puts it: "How do I leave room for other things at the table, and at the same time find a new path that has relevance?"

I have cited his comments at some length because I believe they speak for many people who are being drawn to a new kind of creative edge. Recently I read in *The Structurist*, a magazine published in Canada, that graphic designers have risen up against sterile corporate modernism and consumer capitalism, and are looking for other ways of practicing their craft beyond that of designing brand-name logos and promoting obsolescence. According to Kalle Lasn, founder and editor of the Canadian journal *Adbusters*, graphic designers want to put design skills to more worthwhile and ethical use than product marketing. Instead of trying to become the next big "it" in the design world, these renegade designers joined up with the anti-globalization movement, wrote a manifesto ("First Things First," published in *Adbusters* in 1999), and declared their intention to do something more interesting than just speed up the consumer purchasing cycle. They wanted to try a different tack—instead of promoting saleability, to promote sustainability. "You break out of the commercial box and start playing with the ecological and psychological dimensions of the product-in-use," Lasn writes. "It's an extension of your social conscience."

I view all these transdisciplinary creative initiatives and modest proposals for ethical action as small ruptures in the continuity of capitalism. They are the simplest answer to the question, "Where do spiritual and moral values fit in?" As artists, museums, universities, and other cultural institutions engage in a process of reevaluating themselves, they are forming what Jean-Francois Lyotard once called "a new front." This has brought about an astonishing breadth of practice and a new density of interaction with the world. I have long argued for a more balanced, less "object-centered" aesthetics—a tempering of the focus on objects by a focus on relationships—both as a way of challenging the patriarchal order and also of overcoming our obsession with consumption. I am happy to report that there are clear signs the atmosphere has changed, across a wide spectrum of artistic activities and institutions—and that in the last few years, alternative values and new organizing principles have emerged everywhere. The change is now perceptible: after a half-century of purist ideals, art has become purposeful again, valid and useful in ways that transcend the work itself. The field has been fertilized for the return of art's moral authority.

BIBLIOGRAPHY

Acquaviva, S.S. *The Decline of the Sacred in Industrial Society*. Oxford 1979.
Allport, Gordon W. *Becoming: Basic Considerations for a Psychology of Personality*. New Haven and London 1955.
Arendt, Hannah. *The Human Condition*. Chicago 1958.
————. *Men in Dark Times*. New York and Harmondsworth 1968.
————. *Between Past and Future: Eight Exercises in Political Thought*. New York and Harmondsworth 1978.
Aron, Raymond. *Main Currents in Sociological Thought 2: Pareto, Weber, Durkheim*. New York and Harmondsworth 1979.
Ashton, Dore. *A Fable of Modern Art*. London and New York 1980.
Atwood, Margaret. *Negotiating with the Dead*. New York and Cambridge 2002.
Barber, Benjamin R. *Jihad vs. McWorld: How Globalism and Tribalism Are Reshaping the World*. New York 1996.
Barrett, William. *Irrational Man: A Study in Existential Philosophy*. Garden City, N.Y. 1962.
Barzun, Jacques. *The Use and Abuse of Art*. Princeton, N.J., and London 1975.
Battcock, Gregory, ed. *Idea Art: A Critical Anthology*. New York 1973.
Baxandall, Lee, ed. *Radical Perspectives in the Arts*. New York and Harmondsworth 1972.
Beane, Wendell C., and William G. Doty, eds. *Myths Rites Symbols: A Mircea Eliade Reader*. New York 1975.
Becker, Carol, ed. *The Subversive Imagination*. New York and London 1994.
————. *Zones of Contention: Essays on Art, Institutions, Gender, and Anxiety*. Albany, N.Y. 1996.
Becker, Ernest. *Escape from Evil*. New York 1976.
Bedell, George C. *Kierkegaard and Faulkner: Modalities of Existence*. Baton Rouge, La. 1972.
Bell, Daniel. *The Cultural Contradictions of Capitalism*. London 1979.
————. *The Winding Passage: Essays and Sociological Journeys 1960-1980*. New York 1981.
Berger, John. *The Success and Failure of Picasso*. London 1980.
Berger, Peter L. *The Sacred Canopy: Elements of a Sociological Theory of Religion*. Garden City, N.Y. 1967.
————. *A Rumor of Angels: Modern Society and the Rediscovery of the Supernatural*. Garden City, N.Y. 1970.
————. *Facing Up to Modernity*. New York and Harmondsworth 1979.
————. *The Heretical Imperative: Contemporary Possibilities of Religious Affirmation*. New York 1980.

———. and Hansfried Kellner. *Sociology Reinterpreted: An Essay on Method and Vocation.* Garden City, N.Y.1981.

Berman, Marshall. *All That Is Solid Melts into Air: The Experience of Modernity.* New York 1982.

Berman, Morris. *The Reenchantment of the World.* Ithaca and London 1981.

Birnbaum, Norman, ed. *Beyond the Crisis.* New York 1977.

Bornstein, Eli, ed. *The Structurist,* Issue Number 41/42, Saskatoon, Canada 2001-2002.

Bradbury, Malcolm, and James McFarlane, eds. *Modernism.* New York and Harmondsworth 1978.

Brenson, Michael. *Visionaries and Outcasts: The NEA, Congress, and the Place of the Visual Artist in America.* New York 2001.

———. "The Guggenheim, Corporate Populism, and the Future of the Corporate Museum." Essay published by the Vera List Center at the New School. New York 2002.

Burckhardt, Jacob. *The Civilization of the Renaissance in Italy.* New York 1954.

Burridge, Kenelm. *Someone, No One: An Essay on Individuality.* Princeton, N.J. 1979.

Calinescu, Matei. *Faces of Modernity: Avant-Garde, Decadence, Kitsch.* Bloomington, Ind., and London 1977.

Campbell, Joseph. *The Flight of the Wild Gander: Explorations in the Mythical Dimension.* Chicago 1969.

———. Myths to Live By. New York 1982.

Capra, Fritjof. *The Hidden Connections: Integrating the Biological, Cognitive, and Social Dimensions of Life Into a Science of Sustainability.* New York 2002.

Connerton, Paul, ed. *Critical Sociology: Selected Readings.* New York and Harmondsworth 1978.

Conover, C. Eugene. *Personal Ethics in an Impersonal World.* Philadelphia 1977.

Dewey, John. *Individualism: Old and New.* New York 1962.

Diamonstein, Barbaralee. *Inside New York's Art World.* New York 1979.

Durkheim, Émile. *Moral Education.* New York 1961.

———. *Sociology and Philosophy.* New York 1977.

Eliade, Mircea. *Ordeal by Labyrinth: Conversations with Claude-Henri Rocquet.* Chicago 1982.

Enwezor, Okwui, ed. *Documenta 11_Platform 5.* Exhibition Catalogue, Hatje Cantz 2002.

Ferguson, Marilyn. *The Aquarian Conspiracy: Personal and Social Transformation in the 1980's.* Los Angeles 1980.

Fischer, Ernest. *The Necessity of Art.* New York and Harmondsworth 1963.

Fox, Nigel, ed. *Art and Confrontation: The Arts in an Age of Change.* Greenwich, Conn. 1968.

Frankel, Charles. *The Case for Modern Man.* Boston 1959.

Frankl, Viktor E. *The Unconscious God.* New York 1975.

Friedman, Thomas L. *The Lexus and the Olive Tree.* New York 2000.

———. *Longitudes and Attitudes: Exploring the World After September 11.* New York 2002.

Fromm, Erich. *The Sane Society.* New York 1955.

———. *Fear of Freedom.* London 1960.

———. *To Have or to Be?* London 1978

———. *Beyond the Chains of Illusion.* London 1980.

Funk, Rainer. *Erich Fromm: The Courage to be Human.* New York 1982.

Gablik, Suzi. *The Reenchantment of Art*. New York 2002.

Giddens, Anthony. *Capitalism and Modern Social Theory: An Analysis of the Writings of Marx, Durkheim and Max Weber*. Cambridge, England 1971.

Goodrich, Lloyd. Albert Pinkham Ryder. Centerary Exhibition Catalogue, Whitney Museum. New York 1947.

Gottlieb, Carla. *Beyond Modern Art*. New York 1976.

Green, Martin. *The Challenge of the Mahatmas*. New York 1978.

Greenberg, Clement. *Art and Culture*. London 1973.

Haag, Ernest van den. *Capitalism: Sources of Hostility*. New Rochelle, N.Y. 1979.

Habermas, Jürgen. *Legitimation Crisis*. Boston 1975.

Halifax, John. *Shamanic Voices: A Survey of Visionary Narratives*. New York 1979.

Harrison, Jane Ellen. *Ancient Art and Ritual*. London 1951.

Hess, Thomas B., and John Ashbery, eds. *Avant-Garde Art*. London 1968.

Hillman, James. *Inter Views* (with Laura Pozzo). New York 1983.

Hoffer, Eric. *In Our Time*. New York 1977.

Homer, William Innes. *Alfred Stieglitz and the American Avant-Garde*. Boston 1977.

Horkheimer, Max, and Theodor W. Adorno. *Dialectic of Enlightenment*. New York 1972.

Howe, Irving. *Decline of the New*. New York 1970.

Huxley, Aldous. The Human Situation. London 1981.

Hyde, Lewis. *The Gift: Imagination and the Erotic Life of Property*. New York 1983.

Jacobs, Norman, ed. *Culture for the Millions? Mass Media in Modern Society*. Boston1964.

Jaspers, Karl. *Man in the Modern Age*. New York 1957.

———. *Truth and Symbol*. New Haven 1959.

———. *The Great Philosophers*. New York 1962.

———. *Leonardo Descartes Max Weber: Three Essays*. London 1965.

Josephson, Eric and Mary, eds. *Man Alone: Alienation in Modern Society*. New York 1962.

Jung, Carl G. *The Undiscovered Self*. London 1960.

———. ed. *Man and His Symbols*. London 1964.

Kierkegaard, Sören. *The Point of View for My Work as an Author*. New York 1962.

Korten, David C. *When Corporations Rule the World*. Bloomfield, Conn. 2001.

Kramer, Hilton. *The Age of the Avant-Garde*. London 1974.

Kung, Hans. *Art and the Question of Meaning*. New York 1981.

Kuspit, Donald B. *Clement Greenberg: Art Critic*. Madison, Wisc. 1979.

Kwon, Miwon, ed. *Watershed: The Hudson Valley Art Project*. New York 2002

Laing, Ronald D. *The Voice of Experience*. New York 1982.

Lasch, Christopher. *The Culture of Narcissism*. New York 1978.

Layton, Robert. *The Anthropology of Art*. London 1981.

Lifton, Robert Jay. *The Life of the Self: Toward a New Psychology*. New York 1983.

Lippard, Lucy. *Six Years: The Dematerialization of the Art Object from 1966 to 1972*. London 1973.

———. *Overlay*. New York 1983.

MacIntyre, Alasdair. *A Short History of Ethics*. New York 1968.

———. *After Virtue: A Study in Moral Theory*. Notre Dame 1981.

Mander, Jerry, and Edward Goldsmith, eds. *The Case Against the Global Economy*. San Francisco 1996.

Marcuse, Herbert. *One-Dimensional Man: Studies in the Ideology of Advanced Industrial Society*. Boston 1966.

———. *An Essay on Liberation*. New York and Harmondsworth 1972.

————. *The Aesthetic Dimension*. Boston 1978.

Martindale, Andrew. *The Rise of the Artist in the Middle Ages and Early Renaissance*. New York 1972.

Maslow, Abraham, ed. *New Knowledge in Human Values*. Chicago 1971.

Meyer, Ursula. *Conceptual Art*. New York 1972.

Mills, C. Wright. *The Power Elite*. New York 1959.

————. *The Sociological Imagination*. New York and Harmondsworth 1978.

Moore, Wilbert E. *World Modernization: The Limits of Convergence*. New York 1979.

Mullen, John Douglas. *Kierkegaard's Philosophy: Self-Deception and Cowardice in the Present Age*. New York 1981.

Mumford, Lewis. *The Conduct of Life*. New York 1951.

Nagel, Thomas. *Mortal Questions*. London 1975.

Nicolescu, Basarab. *Manifesto of Transdisciplinarity*. Albany 2002.

Nisbet, Robert A. *The Sociological Tradition*. London 1970.

————. *Twilight of Authority*. New York 1975.

————. *Sociology as an Art Form*. London and New York 1976.

Oglivy, James. *Many Dimensional Man: Decentralizing Self, Society, and the Sacred*. New York 1979.

Olson, Alan, and Leroy S. Rouner, eds. *Transcendence and the Sacred*. Notre Dame and London 1981.

Ortega y Gasset, José. *The Revolt of the Masses*. New York 1957.

————. *The Modern Theme*. New York 1961.

————. *Man and Crisis*. New York 1962.

————. *The Origin of Philosophy*. New York 1967.

————. *Velásquez, Goya, and The Dehumanization of Art*. London 1972.

Parsons, Talcott. *The System of Modern Societies*. Englewood Cliffs, N.J. 1971.

Phillips, William, and Philip Rahv, eds. *The Partisan Review Anthology*. New York 1962.

Poggioli, Renato. *The Theory of the Avant-Garde*. Cambridge, Mass., and London 1968.

Read, Herbert. *The Philosophy of Modern Art*. London 1964.

————. *The Role of the Artist in Society*. New York 1969.

————. *To Hell with Culture*. London 1973.

Redfield, Robert. *The Primitive World and Its Transformations*. Ithaca, N.Y. 1953.

Rieff, Philip. *The Triumph of the Therapeutic: Uses of Faith After Freud*. New York 1968.

Riesman, David. *The Lonely Crowd*. New Haven and London 1969.

Rose, Barbara, ed. *Readings in American Art Since 1900*. New York 1968.

Rosenberg, Harold. *The Anxious Object*. London 1965.

————. *The Tradition of the New*. London 1970.

————. *The De-definition of Art: Action Art to Pop to Earthworks*. London 1972.

————. *Three Decades in Art, Culture & Politics*. Chicago and London 1973.

————. *Art on the Edge: Creators and Situations*. London 1976.

Ross, Ralph. *Obligation: A Social Theory*. Ann Arbor 1970.

Roszak, Theodore. *Where the Wasteland Ends: Politics and Transcendence in Postindustrial Society*. London 1974.

Roth, John K. *Freedom and the Moral Life: The Ethics of William James*. Philadelphia 1979.

Ruitenbeek, Hendrik M. *The Individual and the Crowd: A Study of Identity in America*. New York 1965.

Sartre, Jean-Paul. *Essays in Aesthetics*. New York 1966.

Scott, William G., and David K. Hart. *Organizational America*. Boston 1980.

Sedlmayer, Hans. *Art in Crisis*. London 1957.

Sennett, Richard. *The Corrosion of Character: The Personal Consequences of Work in the New Capitalism*. New York 1999.

Severini, Gino. *The Artist and Society*. Harvill Press 1946.

Shils, Edward. *Tradition*. Chicago 1981.

Sholette, Gregory. "Heart of Darkness: A Journey into the Dark Matter of the Art World." In Blake Stimson and John R. Hall, eds. *Visual Worlds*. To be published.

Simmel, George. *On Individuality and Social Forms: Selected Writings*. Chicago and London 1971.

Slater, Philip. *Earthwalk*. New York 1974.

Smith, Huston. *Beyond the Post-Modern Mind*. New York 1982.

Sorokin, Pitirim A. *The Crisis of Our Age: The Social and Cultural Outlook*. New York 1941.

Spaid, Sue, ed. *Ecovention: Current Art to Transform Ecologies*. Cincinnati, Ohio 2002.

Stangos, Nikos, ed. *Concepts of Modern Art*. London and New York 1981.

Sypher., Wylie. *Loss of the Self in Modern Literature and Art*. New York 1964.

Tomkins, Calvin. *The Scene: Reports on Post-Modern Art*. New York 1976.

VandenBroeck, Goldian, ed. *Less Is More: The Art of Voluntary Poverty*. New York and London 1978.

Vasari, Giorgio. *The Lives of the Artists*. New York and Harmondsworth 1979.

Vásquez, Adolfo Sánchez. *Art and Society: Essays in Marxist Aesthetics*. New York and London 1973.

Vries, Gerd de. *On Art: Artists' Writings on the Changed Notion of Art After 1965*. Cologne 1974.

Wallraff, Charles W. *Karl Jaspers: An Introduction to His Philosophy*. Princeton, N.J. 1970.

Weber, Max. *The Sociology of Religion*. Boston 1964.

———. *On Charisma and Institution Building: Selected Papers*. Chicago 1968.

Wilber, Ken. *A Theory of Everything: An Integral Vision for Business, Politics, Science, and Spirituality*. Boston 2000.

Wilson, Colin. *The Outsider*. New York 1956.

Wittkower, Rudolf and Margot. *Born Under Saturn: The Character and Conduct of Artists*. London 1963.

Wolff, Janet. *The Social Production of Art*. London 1981.